WILD
ATLANTIC
WOMEN

WILD ATLANTIC WOMEN

Walking Ireland's West Coast

Gráinne Lyons

NEW ISLAND

WILD ATLANTIC WOMEN
First published in 2023 by
New Island Books
Glenshesk House, 10 Richview Office Park
Clonskeagh, Dublin D14 V8C4
Republic of Ireland
www.newisland.ie

This edition published 2024
Text and illustrations copyright © Gráinne Lyons, 2023

Print ISBN: 978-1-84840-928-6
eBook ISBN: 978-1-84840-860-9

British Library Cataloguing in Publication Data. A CIP catalogue
record for this book is available from the British Library.

Typeset in 10.5/14.5pt Sabon by JVR Creative India
Edited by Emma Dunne
Cover layout and design by Niall McCormack, hitone.ie
Cover and map illustrated by Curlew Cottage Design,
curlewcottagedesign.co.uk
Printed by L&C, Poland, lcprinting.eu

New Island Books gratefully acknowledges the financial support of
the Arts Council/An Chomhairle Ealaíon.
New Island Books is a member of Publishing Ireland.

10 9 8 7 6 5 4 3 2 1

CONTENTS

PROLOGUE:
BANBA'S CROWN

Malin Head, County Donegal

It's four days past midsummer and I'm standing on the cliff edge at Malin Head in County Donegal. There's a sheer drop beneath me and the wind is full of salt. This is Ireland's northernmost point. Beyond lie the islands of the North Atlantic, the Outer Hebrides, Iceland and, finally, the edge of Greenland, covered in Arctic ice. But before all that is this smudged line of horizon, where the sea and sky have merged. I pull my hood up around me, try to spot basking sharks in the water. Listen to the churn of the ocean as it washes the rocks.

I'm at the end of a journey, of a series of walks I have taken along Ireland's western coastline, county by county, from the bottom of Ireland to this northern tip – a route known as the Wild Atlantic Way. It's a coastal pathway that was once, in my mind, connected to rugged masculinity: to war and fishing, shipwrecks and exploration – hardy, enduring and untameable. But just over three years ago, I started exploring a quieter story, one beneath the surface. I began walking – whenever I could – along this Atlantic coastline. I wanted to see if I could unravel how this elemental landscape had informed the lives of the women who had come before me. How they had moved within it, been shaped by it and how, when they had to, they had left it behind.

I had been thinking about these walks for a while. Back in 2016, on the centenary of the Easter Rising, I had visited Cape Clear, Ireland's southernmost island, where I had celebrated the story of my great-grandfather John K. Cotter. Born on Cape Clear, he was a fisherman and sailor who'd taken part in the Howth gunrunning that had brought to Ireland the rifles used in the 1916 Rising. With skills learnt from years as a pilot in Irish waters, he'd steered Molly and Erskine Childers's boat, the *Asgard*, into port, helping unload weapons into the hands of Irish volunteers.

It was only much later, thinking back over that weekend on Cape Clear, that I began to become curious about his wife – my great-grandmother Ellen Cotter. I felt that somehow, in the excitement of finding out about John K. Cotter, her story was one I had overlooked. I began to ask questions. Ellen Cotter, I found out, had been a lacemaker. A woman whose skill with a crochet hook, over a hundred years ago, had allowed her to dodge a life of domestic service. She was to become the first of a series of women in whose footsteps I would tread, tentatively at first, along this western shoreline.

The truth was, when I began to think about walking in this landscape, I was also at a crossroads in my own life. Although both of my parents are Irish, I have always prided myself on being a die-hard Londoner – a reaction, to some extent, to having two Irish parents and such an Irish name. It's something I share with a lot of second- or third-generation Londoners – pride in a city that gave our parents or grandparents opportunity and gives us a distinct identity. But in 2019, things were shifting. London life was becoming harder than it had been and I couldn't seem to work my way through it.

I had just turned forty but was still single and without children, seemingly at odds with the general flow of things around me. While the majority of my friends were busier than ever, balancing motherhood with their careers, I had just become freelance and had more freedom than ever before. I found myself with whole weekends of time that I was struggling to fill, wondering what my next move should be. I felt, in some ways, that I was on a new path – diverging from what I had supposed to be the template of a woman's life. And this all coincided with a shift in my identity too, as I applied for and was newly bestowed, along with 400,000 other British people, with an Irish passport.

Using the story of my great-grandmother as inspiration, I decided to travel along Ireland's west coast, seeking out the paths and stories of different women who once lived along this shoreline – stories that for me, as a member of the Irish diaspora, were as yet unknown. I thought that perhaps investigating their lives through the words they'd left behind, and the scholarship of the biographers and historians who had come after them, might help me make sense of my own life. That learning about these women could teach me an Irish history I had been lacking and maybe point me in the direction I should go next. And so I began this journey – walking along the coastline with the women of the past, and eventually the present, as my guides.

Each chapter in this book tells the story of a woman, distilled into one walk in the West of Ireland landscape which was or is their home. It is a journey through time that moves up the coastline from Ireland's southernmost island of Cape Clear to its northernmost tip at Malin Head. In selecting the women whose paths I walked in this book, I chose people rooted in and connected to this landscape. My own great-grandmother lived a fairly traditional life, but the women that follow are people I consider to be outliers or subversives, to be in their own way 'wild'. They are people who confounded, or are still confounding, expectations of what a woman can do. Somehow, each of them able to navigate the obstacles or boundaries that circumstance and wider society cast their way. Sometimes they did this through guile, sometimes through sheer grit and sometimes through outstanding talent and searing intelligence, outperforming their male peers until their talent could not be denied.

In West Cork, I walked along the shore once trodden by self-taught botanist Ellen Hutchins, who, in the early 1800s, preserved and catalogued the seaweeds of this coastline as nobody had done before. Walking alone, she found escape from a difficult life at home in the beauty of the seaweeds, lichens and mosses of Bantry Bay, laying the foundation for our scientific understanding of the Atlantic shoreline at a time when we were just beginning to study the natural world. On Valentia Island in South Kerry, one hundred years later, lived Maude Delap – a rector's daughter and brilliant scientist. I walked her island home contemplating how, as the twentieth century dawned, in her homemade laboratory, she became the first person in the world to breed jellyfish in captivity, defying stereotypes to become an expert on these beguiling but sometimes dangerous animals.

In North Kerry, I spent time on the Great Blasket Island, once the home of oral storyteller Peig Sayers, where I found myself in thrall to the force of Peig's personality and charm, falling in love, through her words, with the remote island on which she had lived out her days. Finding out that Peig had never intended to spend her life on the lonely Great Blasket but had dreamt of emigration to America, I sought stories of those who had made the transatlantic voyage. In my mother's home county of Limerick, along the banks of the Shannon, I encountered the campaigning fervour of Charlotte Grace O'Brien, who, in the 1880s, sought to improve conditions for the millions of young Irish women who were crossing the ocean on huge liners, seeking a new life in America.

In Clare I walked along the Cliffs of Moher, exploring the story of perhaps Ireland's greatest living writer – Edna O'Brien. Like my own parents, O'Brien has spent most of her life in London, but in the 1970s she wrote an Irish travelogue, *Mother Ireland*, in which she looked at her own relationship with this country. Immersing myself in her life and work, I compared her vision of Ireland from a distance with the one I had grown up with in London and asked why Edna O'Brien, and many other young women like her, had sought to escape.

Moving up the coast, on Galway's Aran Islands I walked the circumference of the smallest island – Inisheer – taking in the extraordinary limestone landscape. There I met traditional knitter Úna McDonagh. In learning how some of those women who stayed in Ireland created an entire industry through the dexterity of their hands, I also found myself thinking about how these islands have often been portrayed as a romantic, rustic place by writers and filmmakers passing through. Back on the mainland, in Connemara, I continued this meditation on how the people of this shoreline have always been portrayed as a little 'wild' as I walked the roads around Roundstone, encountering a true bohemian – the novelist Kate O'Brien, who lived openly as a gay woman in a grand house bought with the sales of novels banned in Ireland for their frankness.

As I headed up towards my father's home county of Sligo, I stepped back further into the more distant past. On Clare Island in Mayo, I explored the island home of 'pirate queen' Granuaile, who dominated the lands around Clew Bay in the sixteenth century – the daughter of a chieftain who lived her life with now mythic potency and force. Her strength inspired me to enter the realm of Irish legend, as I climbed the Sligo cairn in which the Iron Age Queen Maeve of Connacht supposedly lies.

Finally, in Rossnowlagh, County Donegal, I met Dr Easkey Britton, one of Ireland's most well-known big wave surfers, who is also a marine social scientist. Her unique perspective, formed by a deep intimacy with Donegal's sea and shore, opened my eyes to the most pressing issues of this coastline today – of climate change and how we build reciprocity into our relationship with nature and asked me to think about female identity itself.

Walking along the Irish Atlantic shore in the company of these women was an experience more profound than I could ever have imagined when I first set out. Treading their paths, I took inspiration from how they overcame challenges while moving through this unpredictable landscape, with the full force of the ocean on their doorsteps. Immersing myself in the lives of these very different women helped me understand my own, as I saw how their stories wove and interconnected with each other through time and space, united by the constant, enduring presence of the Atlantic coast.

1. SOUTH HARBOUR

Ellen Cotter
Cape Clear Island, County Cork

'Better to be alone than in bad company,' the ferryman says, scrawling across my ticket with a dark-blue biro. We leave the scored cliffs of the mainland behind us and I feel all at once the exhilaration of travel. My anxieties about being alone disintegrate like the clouds above as the ferry cuts through the waves, away from Baltimore Pier and across Roaring Water Bay. From Heir to Sherkin, Calf to Castle, Horse to Long Island, these islands are a landscape unto themselves – rocky, shifting forms that sometimes slope into the sea or are hard braced against it. On board, I hold tight against the rail, looking out for dolphins and seals, until after an hour come the white houses and ragged fields of Cape Clear – a small island five kilometres long and half that wide. Aside from the tiny Fastnet Rock, Cape Clear – or in Irish, Oileán Chléire – is as far south in Ireland as it's possible to go: a place on the very edge of Europe.

I've visited Cape Clear Island once before, in 2016. Back then, along with the rest of my mother's family, I had celebrated the story of my great-grandfather John K. Cotter, a Cape Clear man who had helped unload the rifles used in the Easter Rising. The sea was choppy that weekend, the weather bleak, but the event somehow went ahead. Some of my relatives got up and recited poems that my great-grandfather had written and historian Éamon Lankford had edited for publication. Half of the poems were in Irish, and since I had no idea what they meant, I'd just sat quietly, concentrating on taking it all in – that I was somehow connected to this island I had never before heard of. I have pictures from that trip – the stomach-churning boat over; a rainy walk on the lanes; myself and a couple of rarely seen cousins leaning against a yellow washed wall, pints in hand and knowing looks into the camera. It would be a few years before I'd process what I'd learnt that weekend on Cape Clear and become curious about the story of John's wife – my great-grand-mother, Ellen Cotter. Ellen also had a career, I found out from Éamon, teaching lacemaking here in the early 1900s to the island women in a wooden school near the North Harbour. And so I am back, returning to walk where she walked and to see if I can perhaps find out more about my own connection to this island and her story.

Just past a half-built house, on the South Harbour, three teenage girls sit in a circle. One wears a hoody with her back to the sea and two others face the ocean, escaped perhaps from the summer college where, the campsite owner told me, students come to practise speaking Irish with the ever-patient islanders. The teenagers feel timeless somehow, the latest in a long line of sullen girls who've stared into this water. They ignore me as I walk by, their tobacco smoke hanging listlessly in the air. On my way up to the glen, the path lined with pink fox gloves, spiked heather and yellow broom, I pass the youth hostel in what used to be the old coastguard station, catch a glimpse in passing of a bunk bed through the window and feel a pang of sympathy for the girls behind me. Turning a corner, I leave the harbour, climbing up the lane that I hope will lead me to 'The House of the Glen', as my great-grandfather called it in his verses, in which he and Ellen once lived.

Like the lace she made, my great-grandmother Ellen Cotter's story is thinner and harder to grasp than that of her husband, John, but there are some things I know to be true about her early life: that she was born Ellen Nolan on 8 February 1880, 450 kilometres from Cape Clear, in a place then called Greagh, near the Fermanagh border in what is today Northern Ireland; that her mother was called Mary and had once been Murphy; that her father was called James and that he was a labourer; that Ellen herself taught lacemaking on Cape Clear. Everything else is lost to time, right up until her marriage in 1909 to John. She must have learnt her lace skills somewhere – perhaps in Fivemiletown, not far from where she grew up, or in Lisnaskea, where a school had been started by the local landlord's wife, Lady Erne. In a country ravaged by famine, the ruling British government had jumped on this growing industry, and in the 1890s lacemaking schools were formed all across Ireland by a government project known as the Congested Districts Board, and this is how the school on Cape Clear in which Ellen taught was founded.

She had caught the tail end of the golden age of Irish lacemaking. In 1880, around the time that Ellen was born, a woman making very fine needlepoint lace could save her family from starvation by selling what she had made, her work embellishing dresses across Europe as the middle classes sought to imitate European royalty. I don't know how Ellen Cotter found her way to the school on Cape Clear – whether she met my great-grandfather and followed him here or whether she had moved for the job. I like to think the latter, but however it was, Ellen found herself at the other end of the country from Fermanagh, bringing industry to the women of Cape Clear, training girls used to gathering seaweed and tilling the soil. Lacemaking could be done at home for extra money between the myriad domestic chores women had to do while the men were away at sea – growing vegetables; tending and milking cattle; churning butter; and hand-washing clothes. I read in an article by Thomas Langan about how these projects operated in Mayo that when the lace schools were formed, there had been concerns that such calloused hands wouldn't be able to do fine work, but work they did, here on Cape Clear, under Ellen's tuition. On this island she found herself, ten years into a new century, newly married and walking up this very path to the Cotter home in the glen.

The scent of pine mixes with that of honeysuckle, hidden in a garden somewhere nearby, as I arrive at the cottage teetering above the crescent bay of the South Harbour. Painted white with red wooden shutters on the windows, it's weathered by time. I peer into the window where a row of china knick-knacks – tiny teacups and a porcelain lighthouse – sit, framed by the pink fuchsias that cover the glen. I linger on the road as I take it all in. There's nobody home and I'm secretly relieved. Entering would entangle me in more recent stories, lead me into another narrative and away from this particular past that I'm trying to find. What was Ellen's life like here? It seems to me an impossible feat – raising five children on an island without electricity or running water, tending the garden to grow what vegetables they could, all while her husband was away fishing for days or even weeks at a time.

Today, there are just 125 people on this island, but when Ellen walked here, there were more than four hundred, all making a living from the sea. As I learned from Éamon Lankford's detailed history of the island, Cape Clear and the other islands around it had been a fishing destination since the Middle Ages. Spanish, Portuguese and French ships joined the Irish to harvest the seas of hake, bream, salmon and herring. But it was mackerel and pilchards that made the Cotter family their living, as well as a sideline piloting boats for other sailors around the coastline of Britain and Ireland. Like generations of women before her, Ellen stood here above the harbour, against the winds that push and pull the island on rough days, watching for the Cotter boats – the *Sarah Gale* and *Gabriel* – each of which carried a crew of nine men to fish the waters around Ireland and Britain.

Samuel Lewis, writing in his *Topographical Dictionary of Ireland* in 1837, had described the Cape Clear men as the best pilots on the coastline, wholly employed in fishing. They left home on Monday and Tuesday mornings in the summer and returned on Fridays and Saturdays, spending their time at leisure before going back out on the water again. Fishing was a trade that involved the entire island, including women and children, who would line the pier at North Harbour when the boats came in, gutting and salting the fish into barrels or smoking the herring, pilchards or mackerel in perforated stone structures that were pleasingly named 'fish palaces'. Reading through the treasure of knowledge that is Finola Finlay and Robert Harris's Roaring Water Journal website, I came across a hand-colourised postcard of fish curing on what is unmistakably the North Harbour of Cape Clear from 1906. This is a whole three years before I know for sure that Ellen lived here. A wooden board is set up on barrels upon which the women work on either side, wearing red shawls around their heads. Head to toe in dark clothing and white aprons, the women look clean and industrious as they carry the salted fish back to the barrels lined up by the side of the quay, with the thin-sailed fishing boats behind them. I showed it to my sister and together we wondered if Ellen Cotter knew these women, working fervently on the harbour to pack the cargo coming into port on Cotter boats; if she'd taught them lacemaking, or taught their children, or worked in the harbour herself on days when the catch was large and needed as many hands as could be found.

I turn right onto a narrower sandy path, breathe in the clean air, take a drink of water and look back. I can see the little bell tent I am staying in for a few nights in the campsite on the other side of the horseshoe bay. From here I start to understand the shape of the island – the thin isthmus road that connects the harbours, north and south. I think about how exposed the lives of the women in the photograph would have been – outside almost all of the time. I imagine them packing fish in the harbour wind; controlling children while on the cliffs; tilling the soil with seaweed and sand. The complete control the ocean held of their lives and those of their families. Perhaps these women had indeed learnt lacemaking from Ellen – brought neat baskets of their work to her on the days when they were not covered in blood and oil from gutting, salting and packing fish. A strange life of contradictions, to do both the cleanest, daintiest work alongside the most bloody.

The Irish crochet lace that Ellen taught was simpler than that made in Kenmare or Carrickmacross, but it was still profitable. In Santina M. Levey's *Lace: A History*, she tells how at one time 12,000 women and children in the neighbourhood of Cork alone were employed to make it. It is a bread-and-butter lace in which linen or cotton is woven with a simple hook into decorous motifs of daisies, roses, shamrocks and leaves, used for collars, trimming or cuffs that were exported to Dublin, London and sometimes even Paris. An example lies under glass at the Clear Museum: two frail yellow collars made, not by Ellen, but by Sister Ciarán Ó Siocháin, an islander taught by my great-grandmother as a child, with the nun's picture leaning up against the shelf behind her crocheted work. It frustrates me that there's nothing else of Ellen Cotter left behind, that her life feels so patchy and filtered by time, that I am scrabbling around trying to find evidence. All I really have, aside from birth and marriage certificates, is the one photograph of Ellen that exists, taken with John, supposedly on their wedding day on 19 January 1909, when he was twenty-nine years old and she was twenty-eight – much older than I thought she'd be. The certificate names them as a spinster lace teacher and bachelor fisherman.

In their wedding photograph, the couple are incongruously posed against a painted walled garden in a photographer's studio that I guess must be somewhere on the mainland. Ellen is sitting on a wooden chair with John standing to her left, his hand resting on her shoulder. She's dressed in a prim white blouse that I'd like to think is trimmed with lace at the high collar and cuffs, but the photograph is so blurred that it's impossible to tell. Beneath that hangs a long checked woollen skirt rather than a wedding dress. Ellen stares into the camera – clever eyes and small lips. Her dark hair is arranged in an Edwardian pile on top of her head and a necklace dangles past her waist. Beside her, John K. has sunken cheeks and the stance of an outdoors person, of someone trussed up and uncomfortable. It's far from what we'd think of as a wedding photo today, these two people I'm related to, looking purposefully dignified as they sternly regard the future. I wonder was she pleased, at her presumably late age for the time, to have made a match? Perhaps John was glad to have found her – how many women with her skills would knowingly have signed up for island life?

A dog barks somewhere in the distance as I walk. I come across a well-kept vegetable garden in wooden raised beds and think of Ellen not only tending to the nine children she had on this island but also doing daily tasks to feed a growing family, often while pregnant or breast feeding. Her first child, Catherine, was born in 1910 and was soon followed by another child almost every year: Kieran, May; the twins, Ellen and James, who both died very young. John and Johanna – who was later called Sis; my own grandfather, Denis, and finally Gabriel. Two more children, Eileen and Anne, would follow later. The twins they had lost on this island were remembered and spoken of for years afterwards – the little girl, who it seems they called Clare to avoid confusion with their mother, having died at just two hours old, and the boy, James, at two years.

The soil is thin, and back when Ellen Cotter lived here the only way to fortify this stony ground was to harvest sand and seaweed from the strand and carry it back up the steep cliffs to lay on the fields – a task the women did while the men were away at sea, carrying the kelp in baskets on their backs.

I reach Pointanbullig – a sheer drop. Here the long grass is permanently swept back by the force of the wind coming in from the ocean. In front of me, the outline of the lighthouse on Fastnet Rock is a hazy silhouette against the horizon. An Charraig Aonair, I've read it is called, which translates to 'the lonely rock'. A place so isolated that the children of this island were once taught to include the lighthouse keepers in their nightly prayers. It also has another name – the teardrop of Ireland – since this was the last piece of land so many Irish people saw as they emigrated to build new lives in America. When Ellen stood here in the early 1900s, this sea was full of ships but now it is empty.

Today is a calm day, but still the Atlantic feels all at once terrifying, vast and overwhelming. Ellen must have had a great respect for, a great fear of the sea. I'm glad to turn my back, sit down in the grass and listen to the evening bird song on the cliffs. By the time I take off again, walking back inland, the sun is setting slowly. I turn right onto a narrower, less trodden way. It's more sheltered here and makes me think about what the winter must have been like – cold and bleak and with the full force of gales blowing in over six thousand kilometres of sea. Cut off from the mainland in an age before phones and email, with only the mail boat every few days, life must have felt precarious, relentless and insular, waiting for fishermen to come home from these dangerous waters. But I wonder, too, if living in such an intimate community brought solace. For Ellen, this would have been a place where her neighbours understood the truth of her situation and were as tied to the unpredictable nature of island life as she was. Even passing through as I am, since I got off the ferry yesterday, I have felt strangely held by the island, as if somehow I have become physically part of it, if only for a weekend.

Ellen Cotter spent at least eleven years of her life on this island, and I suspect more. I know that she was here from the time of her wedding in 1909 until she, John and their children left to start a new life in Kerry in 1920. She was forty then, my own age, while John was forty-one. He had obviously worked hard fishing and piloting in those years – as attested to by his being in Howth with the other island men he was working with in 1916. Perhaps by 1920, with a growing family of seven, Ellen and John both felt that it was time to find a home where life would be less of a struggle. Family lore has it that they sailed down the coastline from Cape Clear's South Harbour around the Cork Atlantic coast on a boat loaded up with the children, John's mother and their entire worldly possessions, including a couple of cows.

They spent the next portion of their lives running a post office on the coast road between Sneem and Kenmare, just on the River Blackwater – a place I plan to visit as I head upwards from County Cork into Kerry and where I have a vague arrangement to stay with some family cousins whom I've never met. I feel a little apprehensive about this – meeting and staying with people who are strangers to me, even though it's something I would do for my work making TV documentaries without a second thought. As I follow the track, the bay falling away beneath me, I realise that I have left a level of comfort behind me – that by doing these walks I'm pushing myself in a way that I don't yet understand.

The loop turns inland and I follow the path downhill, over a stone stile and across an old overgrown mass path, trudging across what I have learnt from my walking guide are called cnoicíns – little hills of grass – now gone to seed. I walk like this for another hour, the sun sinking, until at dusk I rejoin the surfaced road that leads me back down to the north of the island. As I cross the final stile, five magpies sit before me in a row, as if from a picture book of nursery rhymes. We stand off against each other for a few moments until I step forward and they scatter. From Cotters, the bar that was once owned by some branch or other of the family, I can hear music playing. For a moment I imagine the island even more full of life. I am transported to Ellen's intrepid journey across the country; her strength in using her great skill with needlework to find her place; her resilience in embracing, then surviving, island life. I follow the sound of the music down to the North Harbour and, with her memory still in my mind, I let the night take me where it will.

2. A REMOTE COUNTRY

Ellen Hutchins
Bantry Bay, County Cork

I arrive back on the mainland with my skin badly burnt, my hair in need of a wash and my nails jagged and dirty. I'd walked off my night out at Cotters by exploring the other side of Cape Clear and in celebration had swum in the South Harbour at low tide. Now I nurse the remnants of my first ever jellyfish sting, feeling a little stupid but also that I'm learning a bit more about the Atlantic waters and, perhaps, about myself. On Baltimore Pier three women from Dublin stop to ask me about parking and share my disbelief that it's entirely free, for as many days as their island adventures might take. 'You're in a different part of the world now, girls,' a man in earshot declares from his white van as they park up. I drive on to Skibbereen where, washed and rested, I plan my next walks. They will be in the steps of another Ellen – this time Ellen Hutchins, Ireland's first and most prolific female botanist, whose background and life experience was vastly different to my great-grandmother's.

Across the heath and blanket bog of the lower Coomhola mountains, I spend most of the next day walking, climbing steadily across the fields with horseflies circling my ankles, until I can see the entirety of Bantry Bay, across to Glengarriff and the Beara Peninsula. In the early 1800s, Ellen Hutchins spent hours tramping these remote expanses, gathering plants from the shoreline and mountains and becoming the greatest Irish marine botanist of her age. She was one of the first to study the natural life of this Atlantic landscape and her work is intrinsic to any understanding of it. In the nineteenth-century books in which the flora and fauna of Ireland were first catalogued, you'll see her name again and again – next to the seaweeds, mosses, liverworts and lichens that she painstakingly collected.

Waking early again this morning, I now tramp along a narrow country lane outside Bantry that I'm hoping will lead me eventually towards the shore. It's what my father calls a soft day. Moisture is heavy in the air and the hills around are covered in mist. The rain hits my hood in huge daunting drops as I crouch to tighten the laces on my walking boots. I think of the guests in the four-star hotel opposite the trailhead, still asleep in their crisply laundered beds, and wonder how long the rain will keep up. Unsure of my bearings, I've taken a chance following a signpost to Dromloch. It's quiet here, the verges fringed with purple foxgloves and yet-to-fruit blackberries. On either side of the lichen-spotted walls lie tufty, boggy fields. I smell the grass in the damp air and am all at once happy to be outside in nature, despite the rain, walking until I come across the sign that'll lead me to Mass Rock – an isolated spot where people once gathered in penal times, when celebrating Catholic mass was forbidden. Beside Mass Rock, I read, there is also a shrine, Lady's Well, where the water is reputed to have healing qualities. After that the trail should take me down to the shoreline of Blue Hill, where Ellen Hutchins once walked, gathering the seaweed specimens that would become her life's work.

I'd not heard of Ellen Hutchins until a year ago, when in my flat in London I began to plan these walks along the Irish west coast. But the more I read about her, the more fascinated I become with this person who, from her late teens until her death just before the age of thirty, both identified and recorded over 1,100 species of plant along this stretch of Bantry Bay. Her story captivated me, and not only because it mirrored my own growing fascination with this landscape. The deeper I explored Ellen Hutchins's own letters (held in the Wren Library of Trinity College, Cambridge), the research of M. E. Mitchell of University of Galway, and the tremendous knowledge of her three times great-grandniece Madeline Hutchins, the more I grew to know someone of an incredibly resilient nature – a woman who had used her intelligence to cope with what must have, at times, been an intense and even lonely existence.

As a member of Ireland's land-owning class, I'd at first assumed that Ellen Hutchins lived in cosseted privilege, but as her story began to surface, I came to empathise with a person whose life was marked by both her own illness and a duty to care for others. Ellen Hutchins was the second youngest of twenty-one children, of whom only six had survived into adulthood. Her magistrate father died when she was two, and with her sister Katherine having passed away two years later, this left Ellen the only sister of four brothers who had begun to war over their father's inheritance. She had little choice but to stay at home, nursing her frail mother and youngest brother, Tom, who was paralysed after slipping on ice as a child and liked to have her always near to write for him and make him comfortable.

I follow the pilgrim path to Lady's Well that the sick once walked in the hope of being cured, take a right over a stone stile onto a trail across fields of bog grass grown tall and wild. A small creek of stagnant copper-coloured water runs along the field border to my left, surrounded by pennywort and holly, hawthorn and ash trees. I walk along the border of large dark reeds, over another stile – wooden this time – into the fields where cobwebs are spun across the wet grass. I pass a patch of bog irises – a pure glorious yellow – before trekking into the hills, where gorse fringes a muddy trail leading upwards through rocks and red clay. If I look in front of me, I can see Bantry Bay, still covered in mist.

When Ellen Hutchins lived here, Bantry was a prosperous fishing town with a large population that was expanding as the Napoleonic Wars of the early 1800s created demand for cattle farming across County Cork to feed the army and navy. The Hutchins family were landed gentry who seem to have had numerous small estates, even though they rented the home they lived in at Ballylickey from Lord Kenmare. Although Protestant landlords, they were sympathetic to Irish interests – Hutchins's father, Thomas, was vocally opposed to the penal laws of the 1700s that had forbidden Catholics from landownership, schooling and worship. Her eldest brother, Emanuel – a complex character with whom Ellen Hutchins had an up and down relationship – was a friend of Irish rebel Wolfe Tone, whom he'd met studying law at Trinity College Dublin. Ellen Hutchins would have been just eleven when the ships of Wolfe Tone's failed rebellion of 1796 sat waiting in Bantry Bay.

Society was divided in a way that meant that while Ellen Hutchins walked the mountains and shores around Ballylickey House looking for specimens, across these brambled and thorny-gorsed hills, local tenant farmers were walking to a place where they could practise their religion in what I am guessing was an open secret. On the website Holy Wells of Cork and Kerry, I came across a drawing from 1820, which the author said was from the Bantry House Archives, of the Lady's Well pilgrims making their rounds around the well and the Mass Rock, their tents pitched in a nearby field and the crowd so big that everyone in the locality must have known it was a place of worship. I come across a gate that has been painted silver. Knowing I must be near, I hesitantly open it and walk down some stone steps, where I find myself rewarded by the grotto of Lady's Well. Across tiered rocks, where people once gathered, there are now dozens of statues lined up in a row – mostly of Mary – some bronze, some clay, all with their colours fading, their blue and cream robes mottled and weathered. Sometimes, in between them, is the Child of Prague or Saint Bernadette, along with glass vases and jars that visiting pilgrims or children have filled with flowers.

Exposed to the elements like this, some of the statues have cracked into pieces and are leant up against the rock in fragments. They remind me of something you might see in an archaeological museum – torsos, heads and bases in a line. Above, on the higher rock, a larger life-size statue of Mary looks down upon all – a red sacred heart painted on her chest. I don't really know what I was expecting, and I'm delighted by the shrine, although when younger I think I might have been uncomfortable. As a child I adored Mary, encouraged via a variety of metallic badges given out for good behaviour by the nuns at the East London convent my sister and I went to for primary school. But as the years passed, the badges were thrown out, and as I moved into adulthood I began to question why the model of the perfect mother, of the perfect woman, also had to be completely chaste.

But here in the hills of Bantry, surrounded by reeds and rocks and grass, the worship of Mary feels right somehow – in tune with an older, more natural force of remembering, of continuity and ritual. Ellen Hutchins must have known about the Mass Rock, walking as she did daily among the fields and shorelines. Looking for flowers and ferns, she would often walk great distances and I'm sure was well-known by the local farmers.

'I am quite strong and out and about before 7 o'clock in the morning with the workmen,' she wrote to her friend and fellow botanist Dawson Turner. 'I sometimes think you would be amused to see me among a dozen mountaineers, some of them wild enough like goats. I envy their spirits and activity, poor and ragged as they are.'

I find her envy of these local workers that she met on her walks interesting – they clearly had a vitality that Hutchins admired, despite her seeing them as poor and ragged. And of course, I have to wonder, what did they make of her, these apparently goat-like people? A fellow lover of the land, who understood the natural rhythm of nature as it moved around her, or an odd, quiet presence in the fields?

The water in the little domed Lady's Well itself looks surprisingly clear, a mug laid alongside it. People have supposedly been healed by the well, diseases said to vanish when the water is drunk. The legend is that an eel lives within the well and, when spotted, has curative powers. In the Schools' Collection, made up of copybooks collected from schoolchildren across Ireland in the 1930s by the Irish Folklore Commission, one child tells how people came here in August on the Feast of the Assumption to be cured, leaving their crutches and sticks behind. I decline to take up the cup and drink some of the water, afraid it might be contaminated by insecticides, although I am tempted. Perhaps it might inspire visions, bring me unknown insights or at least ease a restless mind? A few weeks later, around a breakfast table in Lahinch, a fellow traveller will tell me how a well in Kerry that was traditionally said to cure madness genuinely did – when examined by twenty-first-century scientists, the water contained tiny traces of lithium.

I exit the well back through the metal gate, rambling across another field until I come to the main road, where I pass an abandoned house, smothered by fuchsias, in which plates are stacked in a dirty window. I take a left along a narrow tree-lined lane – what I guess must be the curved road to Blue Hill, marked only by a sign to a water treatment plant. At the end of the road, a small bay opens before me, deserted except for a woman sitting alone in her car. I wave through the side window to ask her the name of the beach.

'We just call it the airstrip, but it's pretty enough,' she says. 'You can walk along there.' She points to my right, rolling up the window before I can ask more. I'm left with a sense of unease, as I walk towards the shore, for having disturbed her quiet moment of solitude. Who knows why she has come here to think. I look at my trail notes again and decide that this must be Blue Hill – the hills around the town do indeed look blue on this overcast day. Or is the Blue Hill the mound behind me, covered in trees, which I have learnt from my notes is called a drumlin?

Treading my way along the shingle, Whiddy Island opposite me, I look for the seaweeds that Hutchins devoted the majority of her life's work to. I come across a line of compass jellyfish washed up on the sand – the first a small shrivelled tail-less thing, glinting so brightly that it looks almost painted. Further along the sand they get bigger until I find a true beauty, its transparent body glowing orange. Its four frilled arms are spread out languorously on the white and grey sand, coiling at the tips. My upper arm still smarting from my ill-fated swim on Clear, I circle it, both fascinated and repelled, as once Ellen Hutchins must have done here in her playground, an inter-tidal world of mermaid's hair and other seaweeds that she sought to preserve and understand.

Hutchins had been encouraged to take up botany by a family friend, Dr Whitley Stokes, a professor of physic – meaning medicine – at Trinity College Dublin. Hutchins had stayed at Stokes's home in Dublin as a sickly teenager at school. Around 1804, when she was nineteen, she was called back to Ballylickey House to take care of her mother and brother. Dr Stokes, observing that Hutchins's life in Bantry was rather isolated, suggested she take up his own hobby of botany, thinking it would give her both time out of doors and an interesting occupation indoors. And so she did – collecting and preserving with the zeal of the converted. In just two years of her botanical career – between the ages of twenty and twenty-two – she found at least seven species new to science. Over the next eight years, she would find many more and produce a catalogue of over one thousand species of plants in the Bantry neighbourhood.

The more I learnt about Ellen Hutchins's life, the more it became clear to me why she worked with such fervour. She needed a distraction from looking after sick relatives, her own continual ill health and dealing with family strife – a way to see herself as a person apart from the struggles at home. Though plagued with headaches and what seems to have been some kind of abdominal or liver complaint, I like to imagine she decided that, despite all her woes, she would not be helpless. That she'd be active and make the most of her free time on the days that she was fit and able. In a series of letters that – many months after my walk – I was kindly given access to by Madeline Hutchins, I gained an insight into life in the Hutchins household. From the very first letter in 1804, when Ellen was just nineteen years old, there is talk of court cases and 'open war' over money and land disputes between her brothers Emanuel, who was fourteen years older than her, and Arthur, the second oldest. We don't know the exact source of the dispute – it might have been to do with their father dying without a will – but however it came about, it continues year after year throughout the letters.

By 1809, Emanuel – a complex character by all accounts – comes to believe that his family are conspiring against him.

Hutchins clearly loved her oldest brother very much, but relations were sometimes strained. A family friend, Thomas Taylor, later wrote that Emanuel's behaviour was 'such that for the honour of humanity I am glad I can persuade myself that it can only be attributed to insanity'. Emanuel was an intriguing man, with his early association with Wolfe Tone, a difficult relationship with money, and careers as both a barrister and, later, a racehorse breeder in Limerick. He would eventually die in Damascus at the age of seventy on a mission to bring back Arab thoroughbreds.

The letters Ellen Hutchins wrote to him and to her youngest brother, Sam, provide a snapshot of her thoughts and daily life. The overall impression is that Hutchins was sometimes put in the position of peace-broker within the family, conveying both Arthur's and her mother's thoughts and feelings to Emanuel. 'Neither Mother or I closed our eyes all night, she spent most of the night crying,' she writes, 'everything torments us both.' Although we only have Ellen's side of the correspondence, it's clear that she received letters full of blame, harsh words and anger from Emanuel and also sometimes responded in kind herself. 'I am between love and anger,' she signs off one letter in October 1804.

Two years later, their mother, Elinor, dictated a letter for her daughter to send to Emanuel. 'You know very well I have no friend that I could ask to do anything for me,' it reads, 'there is no woman on the world more helpless and friendless than I am.' The Hutchins family were dependent on the rental income from the tenants on their lands, as well as a fishing business. It's clear in the letters that these tenants were also sometimes unhappy – there were skirmishes and cattle killed on some land around Berehaven. As I read, money seemed tighter than I had first thought, or it may be that the arguments around inheritance meant money was being closely monitored. Hutchins herself relied on her mother's income – she writes that she cannot afford botanical books and, perhaps tellingly, no portrait of her exists.

Walking here on these beaches of Blue Hill, Snave and Whiddy Island and in the hills and mountains around Bantry Bay was Hutchins's escape from her troubles. She often walked alone, the hem of her long skirts becoming trimmed with sand and salt as she crunched her way over the tiny stones – some black like coal, some carboniferous grey, others striped with white or containing patches of quartz. The tide is receding now and left behind are threads of neon-green seaweed, so vibrant and alive that no camera can truly capture their colour. Hutchins spent hours exploring the coastline around Bantry in her boat, sailing from the small cove at Ballylickey House. Slowly, she began to see the Atlantic landscape in a new way – as a place of as yet undiscovered beauty.

Sometimes accompanied by a servant girl or boy who carried her boxes and baskets, Hutchins would gather the specimens, make a note of where she found them and then, once home, begin the painstaking work of drawing watercolour illustrations of the seaweeds. She did this as quickly as possible to capture them as fresh, before pressing the plants for preservation. The collections of her drawings in the archives at Kew show that she was astonishingly accurate, and she even speaks in letters of how a little local girl she had brought with her tried to pick one up, thinking that it was the real thing.

Ellen Hutchins had inadvertently struck gold – the climate here around West Cork is slightly warmer than the rest of Ireland, due to the currents of the Gulf Stream, and so is unique in its marine algae. In these long-sheltered inlets of Bantry Bay, the seaweeds are protected from the white waves of Atlantic storms and so grow to huge sizes. I am surprised myself by the variety of seaweed I see as I walk – hairy trails of bleached gutweed and strands of bladderwrack lie on the colourful stones of the shoreline as if posing to be collected and drawn, and I find myself almost envious of what must have felt like a true and clear purpose – to collect and then study each of these wonders.

As her twenties progressed, and helped by the huge variety of life on this shore, Hutchins's stature as a field botanist grew. Soon she became one of the foremost collectors of marine flora and fauna in Ireland, sending out parcels of tenderly preserved specimens and meticulous watercolours to the botanists of the age, scattered across Ireland and Britain – including Dawson Turner, Whitely Stokes, Lewis Dillwyn, James McKay and William Jackson Hooker. Her specimens still exist in Trinity College's herbarium in Dublin and the Natural History Museum in London. Hutchins unexpectedly found herself a remote agent of the enlightenment mania to find, preserve, catalogue and name everything in sight – from plants to animals to the very clouds above us – creating the foundations of modern science a half-century before Darwin would claim his theory of evolution.

As someone who has lived their whole life in the city, I'm struck by the beauty of this small bay outside Bantry, of what is, after all, just the everyday churn of the sea. I'm starting to feel something like rebalancing in my head as I walk and work the geography of Ellen's life out. Leaving the beach, I head up onto the airstrip that the woman in the car mentioned. A child's red bicycle lies on the ground, although its owner is nowhere to be seen. Away from the shore, this feels like a liminal, nowhere place. Who, I wonder, is making use of this cement strip – a remnant of the 1970s, now covered in dried brown grass and weeds? The white markings down the centre and a large '25' are becoming overgrown. A sign warns me not to breach air safety regulations by walking on or near the runway, but I am doubtful we'll see a flight today, or this year or even this decade. Another sign, placed there by a pharmaceutical company, warns that I am trespassing at my own risk.

Beyond the airstrip, the shoreline continues. My walk becomes ever slower as, inspired by Ellen Hutchins, I stop to look up the seaweeds I encounter. Here, yellowed channelled wrack lines the beach, and under the surface of the sea I imagine that, unseen, the kelp forests begin, their long brown fronds washed up on the shore. I didn't even know there were such things as kelp forests until last night, when, walking around Bantry town, I noticed a flyer in a shop window. Sun faded and stuck up with tape that was lifting at the edges, it protested a plan to harvest the wild kelp from the ocean floor. The plan is to industrially cut it from the sea bed – over 1,800 acres of it – and process it to make pig feed. Kelp, I read, absorbs five times more carbon than land-based plants and helps to absorb the impact of wave action, making it a defence against the storm surges created by climate change. I had thought about it before I slept, how Hutchins's work was the start of this understanding of how our planet works, of the danger we are putting it in.

One of the men to whom Hutchins sent specimens, Dawson Turner, who lived in Great Yarmouth in Norfolk, became her closest friend and they would exchange more than 120 letters. In 1809, he asked her to prepare a catalogue of all the plants of her neighbourhood for the newly formed Linnean Society of London, named after the inventor of taxonomy – Swedish naturalist Carl Linnaeus. As they were difficult to observe, marine plants, mosses and lichens were then an overlooked branch of botany, lacking the glamour of the exotic floral specimens from across the British empire that people in London bought from illustrated books to show off at their parties. But Ellen Hutchins found fascination in them and made huge breakthroughs, undertaking this catalogue of Bantry Bay's native species with meticulous care. She described Dawson Turner's request for a catalogue of plants as the best prescription she could have received, and walking here, becoming familiar with the flora and fauna of this shoreline through Hutchins's work, I begin to feel she was right – walking in nature is also, I'm starting to realise, providing me with a remedy I did not know I needed.

The men of science that Hutchins wrote to obviously wondered about this young woman who sent them endless specimens for their books. Welsh botanist Lewis Dillwyn and architect and botanist Joseph Woods visited Ellen Hutchins in 1809, and Dillwyn wrote afterwards to Dawson Turner that 'Miss Hutchins is a very sensible, pleasing, square-made and tolerably good-looking woman of about thirty years old.' In fact, she was twenty-four at the time. 'She naturally possesses very strong senses and pleasing unaffected manners,' he went on. 'Such is Miss H's liberality that we came away loaded with her duplicates. I think Woods is enraptured of her and I have very rarely met with any person equally sensible and interesting.' The two men declared her the best botanist they had ever met.

Joseph Woods, Dillwyn's friend who took a fancy to Hutchins, was actually only one year older than her. He wrote of her admiringly in his journal as earnest and incredibly skilled in the study of natural history. It's appealing to imagine that family friend Tom Taylor, whom she mentions in letters to her brother Sam, might also have been a match, but in truth, it's only my own speculation – we have no record of any suitors. With her nursing responsibilities, ill health and a family in disagreement, not to mention Ballylickey's remote location, perhaps socialising with other young people was something she hadn't the time, resources or energy to pursue?

After all, she was by now consumed by her botanical work and gaining recognition for it too – in April 1807, despite their strained relationship, she asked Emanuel whether she should allow Dawson Turner to publish her name in print as the discoverer of a new species. He must not have replied and she chases him, twice in a month, through their younger brother Sam. It's hard not to become frustrated reading these letters, given that we now know her to be one of Ireland's foremost field botanists, but eventually there was a reply, as Hutchins wrote to Turner in December of 1807 to let him know that her name could be published alongside those specimens she had discovered. Eventually several species – including mosses, lichens, liverworts and seaweeds – would be named after her.

But despite being professionally at her peak, Hutchins's life at home was becoming more and more miserable. Emanuel continued to believe that she and her mother were conspiring with his brother Arthur against him. Hutchins sought peace walking this shore-line as her world began to fall apart. Only in her early twenties, she spent the whole of the summer of 1808 wracked with headaches and in 1809 complained of sickness again. Her mother's condition also began to worsen. Four years later, when Hutchins was twenty-seven, she and her mother moved from the house at Ballylickey to an inn at Bandon, today an hour's drive away, so that her mother could receive better medical care, although it's tempting to speculate that Emanuel might have ousted them from the family seat. Hutchins described her situation to Dawson Turner as one of utter misery but, discreet as ever, did not explain why.

Amidst the turmoil, in her letters to Dawson Turner, the man who had provided her with the great undertaking of cataloguing Bantry's shoreline, I feel her striving to stay upbeat and can-do, despite her circumstances. I read her words as both grateful and modest – making light of her own achievements. Although their relationship grows in intimacy across the years, Hutchins is careful not to overstep the mark of friendship, often signing off with an additional enquiry after Turner's wife. Only occasionally are there glimpses of someone whom I see as caught in internal strife. In one letter, she tells Turner how she sometimes walks 'in the delightful softness of the night', enjoying silence and solitude by the seashore or the river to calm herself after the stress of the day. I wonder if, perhaps, Hutchins was someone with two different identities: as dutiful and patient as she could muster indoors, and out here in the open her wild self – a person whose fervour for collecting was born not just of curiosity but of necessity, of an innate desire for freedom and hunger for knowledge. What might have happened if she had been in better health? Might she have travelled to see Turner in Yarmouth? Might she have met Woods again in London – seen the great house he was said to be designing for his uncle in Stoke Newington, not far from my own London flat? Might she have even met William Jackson Hooker and become the wife of the first director of Kew Gardens?

But my imagination is running away with me, and I have to question my own motivations in matchmaking for Ellen Hutchins in this way. Why am I insisting that satisfaction in life must come from a romantic partner? Am I projecting my own beliefs onto a woman who, although she rarely met them, did have companions as part of a likeminded community of botanists – whom I begin to imagine as something like the early pioneers of the internet – together spinning a web of learning as they corresponded in their earnest study of the natural world?

Hutchins also often spoke of the plants she collected as her 'friends' – these native seaweeds, lichens and liverworts of Cork that I see all around me giving her purpose and joy in a world where she was often in physical pain, as well as dispirited by her troubles at home. It's the final hour of low tide now, and I follow the path of the sea around to the outskirts of Bantry town, speeding up as I cross the shingle, afraid of getting cut off by the tide as people often do. At the slipway that leads down from the pier, I turn up into the town and back towards the hotel where I began. Aside from the woman I spoke to in her car, I have been alone on my walk here along the shore at Blue Hill, as I was yesterday when I walked across the hills of Coorycommane. Hutchins wrote to Dawson Turner of the beauty of walking alone:

> The world felt light and full, ranging over the heath. Here I find advantage in such a remote country, that one can ramble about as one wants. Where else could I be left alone to ramble among the rocks and mountains?

I am beginning to embrace the freedom of walking alone too on these hills and shorelines, of being in nature and not meeting another person for hours and hours. On Cape Clear I had felt nervous about being by myself. I hadn't yet understood something that Ellen Hutchins clearly did – that when you walk alone you are free of the rest of the world, of other people's expectations or opinions. I seem to be losing the watchfulness of the city and I am beginning to properly enjoy myself, to revel in the fact that when I am walking, nobody knows where I am or what I'm doing. This realisation continued today on the shoreline, as looking and learning about the seaweeds through Ellen Hutchins's curiosity, I began also to appreciate the beauty she saw all around her as she walked – to understand how happy she was here in her solitude.

*

From Bantry I travel on, passing by the Ardnagashel estate where Hutchins spent the last few months of her life, taken care of by her brother Arthur and his wife, Matilda, in a house on the shore. Today it is part of a large complex where tourists can rent cottages, around which is a forest planted by Arthur that includes rare trees such as the orange-barked Chilean myrtle, which was probably provided by Kew Gardens – no doubt through Ellen Hutchins's connections. It was in this house on the shore that Ellen Hutchins died, a month before her thirtieth birthday, possibly of liver disease which was being treated with mercury – in itself poisonous. In her dying days she wrote to her true friend Dawson Turner, thanking him for his letters, which she had read with tears of gratitude and affection.

I stop for the night in a cabin in the woods just beyond Ardnagashel, in the woods of Glengarriff. The name translates from the Irish An Gleann Garbh to 'the rough glen' – a rugged place where the Caha mountains meet the sea. The cabin is in the nature reserve that preserves these oceanic oak forests where, despite frequent rain, frost is rare. Atmospheric and damp, the climate here is a couple of degrees warmer than the rest of Ireland, 'almost subtropical' I read in a visitor guide, a phrase I find hard to equate with Ireland, but the evidence is all around me – mosses, ferns and liverworts spread luxuriously across these alluvial forests. Hutchins' Hollywort, a delicate and rare toothed leafy liverwort, grows here, deep in the woods, named after Ellen Hutchins by William Jackson Hooker.

The place I'm staying in is owned by Audrey, an artist who sculpts horses and wolfhounds, currachs and Celtic knotworks – souvenirs of Ireland that her husband then casts in bronze. When I arrive I'm talking too much from the force of a day spent inhabiting another person's life; perhaps I have caught some of Ellen Hutchins's own pent-up agitation. Audrey shows me to my tiny wooden cabin, pointing out a hammock hanging between two trees, and for the rest of the afternoon I experience true tranquillity, dozing in and out of sleep. I feel safe and protected, surrounded by the day-to-day life of the smallholding – the vegetable garden, a tethered goat called Heather, two cats and a cockerel who steps up to the fence every time I pass by, shaking his wattle aggressively as he crows to guard his anxious hens. The cabin itself is a wooden structure something like a shed propped up on concrete stilts, with electricity and net curtains on the front windows to make it more homely. The beds are clean; I have no neighbours and I find myself completely at ease.

Inside as night falls, so the rain starts. The air becomes heavy and humid and soon I'm surrounded by the smell of damp wood from the forest outside. I pass the time looking at Hutchins's drawings online, the unfamiliar Latin names somehow soothing: *Conferva pedicellata*, *Fucus asparagoides*, *Conferva brodiaea* – watery plants chosen and plucked from their homes by Hutchins to forever represent their entire kind, egg-shaped purses and flat, grassy fronds intertwining so that they reminded me of other-worldly life forms. The perfect specimens. Cleanly drawn and precise in their details, they embody a scientist's desire for order in an overwhelming world, a dissection of chaotic nature. On my digital screen, I see how Hutchins worked – each part of the plant in question individually separated and drawn in cross-section: a leaf; a detail of a frond; a spindly stem; a branch heavy with fruit. There's a surrealistic quality to her drawings in the way each of the plants has been excised and examined apart from its whole. Body parts suspended and captured in the same way that the French surrealist artists Breton and Man Ray dismembered the women they photographed or cut from magazines. There's something soothing – tranquil even – about this beautifully illustrated world in which every plant and flower has its order and place.

As I drift off to sleep, deep in the forest, it occurs to me that my search for Ellen Hutchins's life has mirrored her personality, her experience easily missed to all but the curious – just like the quiet non-flowering seaweeds, mosses, liverworts and lichens she collected. She has opened up a new world for me – of the huge variety of species here on the coasts of West Cork that I begin to see as she once did: studded with the treasures of nature. I admire her greatly – not only for her huge contributions to our scientific understanding of this coastline, but also for finding a way, through her love for botany, to freedom from her day-to-day oppressions. Her life was a far cry from those of the island women of Cape Clear, carrying baskets of kelp up the cliffs to use on their potato gardens, but physical comfort doesn't always equal contentment, and Ellen Hutchins clearly had her own burdens to carry.

In a way, she feels more real to me than Ellen Cotter did. Is it because she left a voice behind, through her letters, through her work? Or perhaps I simply have more in common with her – with her passion for books and learning and getting to the answers? Perhaps she reflects back at me my own educational privilege? She has challenged me, because at first, I think I pitied her. I saw her as a victim of circumstance. I wanted her to marry Woods or Tom Taylor or find some way out of Ballylickey to the scientific community of kindred spirits that she shared her work with and who clearly admired her very much. But the truth is that being tied to this shoreline by circumstance was the very thing that brought her success and that means we still remember her today. Like Ellen Cotter before her, she made the best of the opportunities she had and I wonder if that's what I should take from her story: to find my own path and see where it leads.

3. MISS DELAP

Maude Delap
Valentia Island, County Kerry

I wake early the next morning, a thin dawn light outside. Try as I might, I can't get back to sleep. Perhaps it's being in an unfamiliar place, in an unfamiliar bed, or perhaps it's something else, but the determination that I had last night seems to have withered away and been replaced by uncertainty. On the clifftop at Cape Clear I'd had a moment of wondering if perhaps this is a dangerous thing to do, walking alone in isolated places that I don't know, even though these are mapped trails that people locally must know like the backs of their hands. There's nothing to be afraid of here, or at least no more than back home in London, so what is it that's bothering me? As the forest awakens around me, I try to work the feeling out.

Perhaps when I'd planned this journey it was a jaunt of sorts, and now I'm coming to realise that walking in the footsteps of these women requires me to fully commit – to think properly, to walk properly. And also to take a risk, as an English person writing about an Irish history that I'm learning piecemeal, as I go. Perhaps also, Ellen Hutchins's story has touched a nerve with me – her desire to escape home life in her botanical work, to find an order that might hush a restless mind. Am I seeking escape from the expectation of what my own life should or could be? Or am I seeking home? I'm unsure. All at once, I feel like the outside world is too much. I want to stay hidden here in this little cabin in the woods forever, to never go back.

But once I'm on the road, travelling along the Beara Peninsula, my spirit picks up again. In the brightly coloured hill town of Allihies I stay with Irene, whose bed and breakfast bungalow has a cream-painted wall and garden gnomes outside. She's exactly the person I need today, as, with every other guest a German walker, Irene delights in my name – the reaction to which is fast becoming my favourite thing about travelling in Ireland. Almost everyone I meet seems pleased with my parents' decision to give me this name that requires so much explanation in the UK that I use pseudonyms for coffee orders and restaurant bookings. Here, it helps me fit in, makes me feel like family, and with her cropped dark hair Irene reminds me of a cousin or aunt, pampering me at breakfast and making time to chat. She helps me plan a walk in the hills above the town by exactly pre-dicting when the rain will stop simply by looking out at the sea. 'It'll be clear by eleven,' she says, and so I have permission to nap before heading out on a trail covered in ferns and white bindweed that gives way to limestone cliffs and then boggy land.

The abandoned copper mines beneath Allihies mean it's my hardest walk yet – large, unexpected pools of boggy water mean every step must be considered and my socks are sodden by the end. As Irene predicted, the weather moves fast here on the tip of Beara, and by the afternoon, I'm carefree and sunbathing on Ballydonegan Beach beside two little girls who play at being mermaids, stuck to the rocks. I think of them that evening as I pass what's said to be the rocky remains of an ancient goddess of winter – the Cailleach Beara, or Hag of Beara, who turned to stone waiting for the sea god Manannán mac Lir to return.

Through Cork and into Kerry, I make my way across the five great peninsulas that stretch out like arms into the Atlantic. The chain of remote islands that exists along its shoreline fades in and out of view. I begin to learn the islands' shapes and names – the green mounds of Scariff and Deenish, the sharp jut of Skellig Michael. In Kenmare, I stop at the Lace and Design Centre next to the town museum, where I hope to find out more about the crochet lace my great-grandmother made. Behind a glass counter, a fastidious lacemaker named Siobhán shows me the precision of the work that once fed families, describing the different kinds that were made across the south-west of Ireland – Carrickmacross, Youghal, Limerick. Siobhán lingers long on Kenmare lace, the intricate needlepoint for which the town is famous. Finer than the crochet lace I had seen on Clear, Siobhán explains that it can only be made for two hours a day, in the morning, when the light is just right. 'There's a lot of washing of hands,' she tells me, and as I continue on my journey along the top of the Iveragh Peninsula, now on the Ring of Kerry, I think about the parallels between the work of the lacemakers and that of Ellen Hutchins.

Hours of dedication and accuracy as they created their small bundles of fabric or drawings or specimens, making sure everything they did was absolutely exact.

Past Cahersiveen, I cross the thin road bridge that now connects the mainland to Valentia Island. Here, one hundred years after Ellen Hutchins, lived another self-educated scientist – Maude Delap, a pioneering marine biologist who made her early scientific breakthroughs from a house at the harbour's edge in Knightstown. Rather than seaweeds, Delap studied jellyfish. I came to her story through a series of artworks made in the early 2000s by contemporary Irish artist Dorothy Cross. Inspired by Maude Delap's work, she had collaborated with her brother, the zoologist Professor Tom Cross, who was studying the ethereal *Chinorex fleckeri* – a type of venomous box jellyfish – in Queensland, Australia. Together they produced a film, *Medusae*, which wove graphs, notes and drawings from Delap's own experiments with the movement of the box jelly. My interest piqued, I tracked down a copy of *Stars, Shells and Bluebells*, edited by Mary Mulvihill, in which the lives of forgotten Irish women scientists are recalled, including Anne Byrne's writing about Maude Delap. That led me onwards to the work of Dr Nessa Cronin, and soon I found myself completely immersed in all things Maude.

In the village of Knightstown, children are swimming in the harbour. Along the side of the pier, toddlers and their parents dip brightly coloured nets into the dark water. When Maude Delap arrived on this island in 1874, she was just eight years old, the seventh of ten children of the Reverend Alexander Delap and his wife Anna Jane. Born in a rectory at Templecrone, Donegal,

Maude Delap was already used to life on the Atlantic edge, and as she grew, the sea around Valentia would become ever more fascinating to her. Her father, at the age of forty-four, had taken a new position as rector of Valentia and Cahersiveen, a parish that he was proud to say included the far-flung Skellig Islands. Although Maude Delap and her six sisters were not formally educated like their brothers, they accompanied their father, who was a keen amateur naturalist, on his small boat as he made visits, learning the basics of botany and zoology from his practised eye and coming to know the Valentia landscape intimately.

I walk from the harbour clocktower through the village, taking a small detour right down a road where the name Reenellen – the Delap sisters' house – survives on a black and white sign. A memorial to Maude Delap has been placed on the corner – a red plaque shaped like a jellyfish on which her name and dates are marked. At the end of the road, an old grey stone house stands, crumbling, vacant and surrounded by fences and barbed wire. This now abandoned place is where Maude Delap lived with her sisters and mother after her father died, conducting her research in her homemade laboratory, known as 'The Department'. A description of it by her nephew Peter Delap remembers a 'heroic jumble of books, specimens, and aquaria, with its pervasive low-tide smell'.

Maude Delap was in her mid-thirties when she achieved her major scientific breakthrough, as – despite being self-taught – she became the first person in the world to observe the complex life cycle of the compass jellyfish, *Chrysaora hysoscella* (which she called

Chrysaora isosceles), the same species that I think stung me, with its striped body and frilled tentacles. The compass jellyfish provided Delap with her break-through, publishing her findings in *The Irish Naturalist* in 1901. With my own sting only now fading, I'm currently regarding jellyfish with a mixture of wonder and horror, but Maude Delap had no such fear.

I walk around the fenced circumference of this once grand house, its windows cemented up and the view of the harbour going to waste. It's easy to imagine Maude Delap and her two remaining sisters, Mary and Constance, living here in their later years. Sometimes alone, but often with Constance, Maude Delap would head out onto the ocean and use a dragnet to trawl the waters looking for jellyfish and other planktons, which she would then breed in homemade aquariums. Breeding and feeding both compass and blue jellyfish in bell jars, she observed the various medusa and hydra life-cycle stages of these species, providing detailed accounts of their development and feeding habits.

Through Knightstown, past the coffee shops filled with tourists taking afternoon tea, I walk towards Saint John the Baptist, the Church of Ireland building opposite the house which was Maude Delap's child-hood home. Saint John's is classic country church built in about 1860, inside which a man is holding court to two young tourists, explaining the provenance of the church's nineteenth-century stained-glass windows. 'The one on the left is hope,' I hear him say, 'while the cen-tre window depicts charity.' He is in such full flow and they are so engrossed that it seems rude to interrupt. Instead I sit in one of the pews, around which it's easy to imagine the Delap girls spending their childhood, ordering hymn books and gathering flowers for the altar. In the house across the road, Reverend Delap spent his spare time packaging up specimens for the Natural History Museum in Dublin. As they grew, Maude Delap and her younger sister Constance began to follow in their father's footsteps, sending their own finds to Dublin to be catalogued.

The full list of donations made to the Natural History Museum from the Delap family, provided to me by one of the current assistant keepers, Amy Geraghty, makes entertaining reading – from two trout the Reverend Delap donated in 1885 to a loggerhead turtle Maude sent them in 1949. Maude Delap had begun her contribution to the museum's two-million-strong collection with a pill millepede in February 1894, when she was twenty-seven, and was soon sending specimens regularly. A group of Valentia jellyfish and tunicates she donated in early summer 1907 are held there to this day. I had the pleasure, in a secretive strongroom in Dublin where the Natural History Museum's wet collection is stored, of holding these jars of specimens in my own hands. Although many of them seem to have deteriorated over time, the common salps – *Salpa fusiformus* – from 1907 appeared as translucently fresh as the day they were collected, thanks to the liquid spirit in which they've been kept.

As well as her pioneering work on jellyfish, Maude Delap was, in the words of her nephew, 'an old-school Victorian all-round naturalist. A recognised expert on marine biology, she was also interested in the birds, plants and the archaeology of the whole countryside.'

Walking around the island, as I am doing now, he describes how, 'Wherever we went she was instantly recognised and greeted with delight.' Any curiosity discovered by the island people was immediately brought to the reverend's, and then later Maude's, attentions. As the reverend's daughters, Maude and her sisters were also responsible for the Fisherman's Hall – an open house where passing fishermen were given sustenance in the form of tea and buns. For a family of naturalists, it was also a great opportunity to gather new knowledge and specimens from the fishermen who worked upon the ocean daily. Whether from a sailor or on one of her daily excursions, on 22 April 1935, when she was sixty-eight, Maude Delap was to come across her greatest find as a specimen collector: the carcass of a rare True's beaked whale that had been stranded on rocks by the lighthouse – to which I am walking today.

I head down the lane past the Heritage Centre, once the island's school, passing white bungalows on each side. Outside some retirement flats, two old dogs sleep in the sun. One raises his head – the flicker of a memory of having once guarded – before resting back down onto his paws. The lane narrows, becomes overgrown with orange montbretia, purple loosestrife and the usual pink fuchsias. This is my most colourful walk yet, the walls along each side of the road made of thin Valentia slate stacked and topped with dried yellow grass from the hot weather so they look like they've grown hair. At the ruins of an ancient church to my right, two men are unloading a trailer with shovels and a hoe, so intent on their work that I decide to save my visit to Maude Delap's grave for the way back.

Before I came here, I saw Valentia as a remote place on the edge of Ireland, but the more I learn about Ellen Hutchins and now Maude Delap, the more I am beginning to challenge my own ideas of remoteness, of what a remote place really is. While Ellen Hutchins was connected to the urban centres of Dublin and London through her letters, a century later, when Maude Delap was growing up on this island, something was happening that meant that London and New York were not as far away as I had imagined. In 1866, Valentia Island had been connected to the wider world through the first transatlantic telegraph station, where 1,686 nautical miles of copper cables under the ocean linked a tiny fishing village called Heart's Content in Newfoundland with Knightstown. London could communicate with New York within hours. Messages that had previously taken two weeks by boat were now almost instant.

At the same time, because of its unique position on the western seaboard, Valentia was being recognised as a place of meteorological importance. In August 1860, an observatory was set up where weather systems moving in from the Atlantic could be captured, studied and forecast. As the specimens collected by the Delap family mounted, Edward T. Browne, a young marine biologist at University College London, began to think it might be worth investigating the natural world of the island, and so in 1895 and 1896, the Delaps found themselves playing host to Browne and seven other scientists of the Royal Irish Academy while a complete survey of the island was undertaken. Soon Maude and Constance Delap would find themselves being trained in scientific techniques, refining the skills their father had taught them and learning how to capture specimens – a task they undertook with enthusiasm. Their work would become key to the Valentia Island Survey's success – as Dr Nessa Cronin of the Centre for Irish Studies at University of Galway points out, in her research that can be viewed online, there are over forty references to Maude Delap's contribution in the survey itself.

The forested cliff road to the lighthouse, fringed with sycamores, ash trees and alders, feels almost Mediterranean – the sparkling sea in glimpses beneath me and the giant leaves and spiked red flowers of gunnera in the shaded borders. It is easy to imagine Maude Delap walking here with Edward T. Browne. Delap and Browne were both nearing thirty when Browne's survey began – the same age as my great-grandmother when she had married on Cape Clear. The history of the Delap family has it, as recalled by her great-nephew John Barlee in Anne Byrne's chapter of *Stars, Shells and Bluebells*, and confirmed to me by Delap's grandniece Joanne Lee, that working as closely with him as she did, Maude began to develop feelings for Edward Browne.

When the survey ended, she had an excuse to stay in touch, as the Delap sisters continued to collect information and specimens for Browne, who had returned to University College London. I pored over the letters and notebooks she sent him, now stored in the archives of the Natural History Museum in South Kensington, intent on finding evidence of their romance. Instead I found log books: pages of data about jellyfish – how she bred and fed them, records of sea temperature and of her finds. There was, within the dusty boxes, no indication of the feelings that local lore says Browne did not return, for he married one of his colleagues. Nevertheless, the story goes that Maude Delap continued to send him a box of violets on his birthday every year, corresponding with him until his death in 1937.

What I did find in the archives, however, was evidence of Maude Delap's personality. She describes the specimens she is breeding as 'lively little beggars', says of the compass jellyfish she had grown that 'the Beast is beautiful today', speaks of a trip to the island of Little Skellig on 25 May 1907 that she climbed for five and a half hours and the gannets 'were splendid'. Her faint, thin drawings of salps and aurelia – moon jellyfish – also brought me closer to her. Neat, but not too neat, and never truly centred on the page. Next to Browne's own notebooks, which are immaculate and tightly penned, Delap's looser notes feel, to me anyway, driven by something more than precise scientific enquiry – a natural, instinctive curiosity, perhaps, to keep looking, to keep trying until she had fully understood her aim.

The survey had given Maude and Constance a new-found vigour in their studies, and now very much connected to the wider scientific world, Delap published observations of their fieldwork, which examined plankton in Valentia Harbour from 1899 to 1901 and 1901 to 1905. It was also in June 1899 that Maude Delap had her breakthrough in her laboratory work, successfully rearing the compass jellyfish in a bell-jar aquarium and observing its life cycle. The paper she published in February 1901 in *The Irish Naturalist* tells of how she found a damaged specimen of the compass jellyfish on the harbour shore and placed it in an aquarium on midsummer's day, 21 June 1899. The following day it had spawned, and a few days later tentacles had developed.

Over the winter of 1899, Delap writes of how she fed the growing animals with seawater twice a week in a 12-inch bell jar, and by the following May she had reared a mature compass jellyfish. Eventually she struggled to keep it alive due to stormy weather that prevented her from gathering plankton from the sea. The jellyfish's appetite was enormous and she simply couldn't keep up. She describes how it would eat, stretching out its long arms to devour the smaller jellyfish on which she fed it, and I imagine her captivated by this primal boneless creature as she unravelled the mysteries of a lifeform far older than us. Here on the road to the lighthouse, a sign points me to Valentia's tetrapod imprints – marks left behind that show the transition of amphibians from water onto land – but jellyfish have been on Earth for over 500 million years, long before dinosaurs lived here and 200 million years before anything walked on land. Now, with our warming oceans, jellyfish are increasing year on year, while larger mammals decline, and they are inheriting the coast.

I'm now in the part of the island called Glanleam, making my way down a steep hill towards Cromwell Point, on which the lighthouse stands. In front of me in the far distance is the soft rounded form of uninhabited Beginish Island. Helen Richmond, the artist in whose house I am staying just outside Cahersiveen, told me over breakfast how she once camped through a storm on Beginish, in a womb-like one-person tent in which she felt warm and safe while the wind raged. I was glad to find a fellow solo traveller and we'd talked deeply about what life was like down here – about her art, her work with asylum seekers and the variety of people who find themselves stopping in her spare rooms. My three-night stay is unusual, she tells me – most stay for one, some for two, before they head to Clare or Killarney, Dublin or Cork. They can't have time, I think, to appreciate these hairy slate walls of Valentia, weathered into a patchwork of colours – grey and teal, brown and violet.

By 1906, Maude Delap was a recognised expert in marine biology. That year, at the age of forty, she was offered a professional position at the Plymouth Marine Biological Station – a great honour for a woman at that time – but she declined. The story goes that her father reacted with the words, 'No daughter of mine will leave home, except as a married woman.' But looking at the dates, 1906 was in fact the year that the reverend died. Who knows what state the family was in? After her father's death, his widow, Anna, and her three remaining daughters, Mary, Maude and Constance, moved from the rectory to the now derelict house in Reenellen that I visited at the start of my walk. They led a largely self-sufficient life on the island – growing fruit and vegetables, keeping cows, eating carageen moss seaweed and selling gladioli and arum lilies.

Reenellen had neither electricity nor central heating. Their nephew Peter describes a winter visit in which he began to

> fully appreciate their stoic endurance in the huge intractably draughty and damp house with its oil lamps and inadequate turf fires. The ephemeral nature of all our possessions was reinforced by rampant decay; woodworm, damp-rot, moulds and fungi of all kinds were hyperactive. Mice

and cockroaches roistered almost unchecked; these latter serving as a useful deterrent against more finicky visitors.

The sisters continued to wear the Edwardian-style clothes of their youth well into the twentieth century in order to fit into the wider community of the island, where poverty was rife.

Despite, or perhaps because of, their eccentricities, the sisters were well-liked, and they seem to have been, fortunately, amicable. Photographs of Mary, Maude and Constance taken in the 1930s and 1940s show them smiling – obviously at ease in each other's company. Nora Ní Shúilleabháin, a schoolmaster's daughter who grew up with the Delap sisters, is quote by Anne Byrne as describing how these spinsters had defied the stereotypes of the lonely old maid through their passion for the natural world. I find myself, as I walk, falling into a meditation about spinsterhood. How now, over a hundred years later, if I am honest with myself, I have also internalised this old-fashioned stereotype of being left behind, of what fulfilment in a woman's life should be – that I have somehow 'missed the boat' on marriage or children because, for whatever reason, my relationships so far just haven't worked out.

Thinking rationally, I know that this has been out of my control – down to careers, some near misses and some rotten luck, as I had a period of ill health in my early thirties, just around the time my friends were meeting their partners. I also think, perhaps, it's down to the way people meet each other in big cities – using dating apps and judging each other far too quickly. One of the most wonderful things about being able to take this time for myself, to do these walks, in fact, is the relief of not feeling that I should somehow be trying to meet someone on these tedious apps. Statistically, anyway, I know I'm not unusual. In London, over one-fifth of people are now in single households. But when I don't rationalise – when I let my emotions take over – it can get me down, the pressure of it, whether that's internal or from those around me. My friends and family don't mean it, but they can't help but wonder aloud about what is going on with my love life – when will I settle down with the right man? Sometimes I think they want to live vicariously through my stories of awful dates, or sometimes they are kinder, offering to let me know when their recently divorced friends are back on the market. Sometimes I see a tilt of the head and just a kind of curiosity, as if they are trying to work it out.

And if that's a pressure I'm struggling with, then what was it like for women of previous eras? Was Delap's affection for Edward Browne a way of fulfilling some psychological need for a male confidant? Or perhaps the story is exaggerated and they were just excellent colleagues? In truth, Maude Delap could really only pursue her passion for marine biology because she was single. Had she married, a career might have been seen as unseemly. On my visit to the spirit collections of the Natural History Museum in Dublin, keeper Amy Geraghty had told me the story of another great early Irish naturalist, Jane Stephens. She had been on the Clare Island Survey of 1909 to 1911 in County Mayo, an expert in sponges and a member of the museum staff. Due to a marriage bar, which was only repealed in the 1970s, Jane Stephens was compelled to retire in 1920 when she wed the then acting director of the museum, Dr Robert F. Scharff. For many women it might have been a choice between career and marriage.

Maude Delap was past retirement age in April 1935 when, on this very road I am walking, she organised the transportation of the washed-up True's beaked whale to the museum. The huge ferns of the high road I have just walked are replaced by rougher vegetation as I near the shore where the whale was found, the lane flanked by meadow thistles, purple heather and yellow furze. On the hillside above me, there's a line where the forest stops. A sign warns cars to give way to climbing traffic as the road turns into ridged cement – the climb back is going to be steep.

The wind has risen and I zip up my coat against it, pass an old slate house in ruins to my right and a huge rock protruding out to sea on my left, covered in white lichen. This is where I imagine that the True's beaked whale – a rare deep-water species whose skull still sits in the Natural History Museum of Dublin – must have been stranded. The whale was male and already dead when Delap found him, so there was no chance of refloating the animal. Although I know that as a scientist Delap must have killed many specimens to preserve them in their prime of life, it's still a relief that this rare whale was not one of them. The whale was fifteen feet ten inches long. A photograph exists in the Valentia Museum of three boys and four men with it, one of whom is sawing off the head. Delap had been asked by the museum to send them the flippers and skull. The caption scrawled across the photo mentions a man called Mike, who worked at Reenellen, and another called John Dore. It must have been quite an effort to convey the whale along the road I have just walked back up to Reenellen and it is extraordinary to think of Delap, in her late sixties, co-ordinating these men and boys as they transported it, presumably by horse and cart.

Once the whale had been brought up to the house, as instructed by the museum, the Delaps buried the skeleton under the asparagus patch, so that it could rot before cleaning. This is apparently still the most sensible thing to do, should you find a rare whale that has died, Amy told me. It's so the flesh can decompose leaving the skeleton in the correct order.

There are other photographs from the event, with blood on the rocks and the skull, now white and clean, on a table in the garden at Reenellen, a neat hedge behind it. The story, as again told by Anne Byrne, goes that after Maude had sent the skull to the museum, they requested that she also send the bones. She dug up the vegetable patch and duly did so, only for them to write again that the whale's vestigial pelvic bones were missing. The vegetable patch upset for a third time, Maude Delap was sifting through the by now well-fortified earth when a telegram arrived: 'Stop! New York Museum informs us that True's beaked whale does not possess vestigial pelvic bones.'

When I finally reach the shore, the lighthouse directly in front of me, it's high tide. Tiny flowers of borage and bird's foot trefoil appear in the windswept grass as I approach the lighthouse, next to which huge slabs of flat rock point out towards Beginish Island. I speak to the man in the front cabin to find that the lighthouse, now a tourist attraction, has just closed – I missed it by a matter of minutes. 'There's a storm brewing,' he tells me – words so stereotypically what I imagine a lighthouse keeper to say that I'm unsure what to reply. I turn around and sit down, my back against one of the boulders that protect the shore, seeking a moment's rest from the wind that now feels as if it's boring its way through my ears, before I make my way back up to the cliff path.

*

I'm cold by the time I return to Helen's house, and the next day betrays my having overdone it. Confined to bed with what seems to be the start of something flu-like, I'm fed fresh ginger-and-lemon tea by Helen in her home, which doubles as an art studio, I discover that she is an excellent nurse, as by seven the next morning I am up and out to the pier at Bealtra, where a boat takes me out to the Skellig Islands – somehow perfectly bathed in sunlight for the two hours I'm there. Here, in the sixth century, thirteen Christian monks lived in isolation, called to a life of *glas* – green martyrdom. They survived on the eggs of gannets, guillemots and puffins, who have now almost completely taken the islands back, covering them in their nests and droppings.

I had to book weeks in advance for the trip – since *Star Wars* filmed here in 2014, portraying the stone beehive huts as Luke Skywalker's retreat, the carefully co-ordinated boat trips to this UNESCO world heritage site are packed, with only a certain amount of people allowed on the island at any one time. The climb up to the beehive huts – which I'm sure Maude Delap and her father did – is hard but rewarding. Once at the top, tourists from across the globe picnic in the monks' vegetable garden and fall asleep hungover behind the monks' beehives. I imagine the martyred monks climbing the rocks up to the highest point of the island and spreading their arms out to sea as they prayed, believing that they were at the edge of the known world, as close to God as it was possible to be.

By the afternoon, I am continuing my pilgrimage through the life of Maude Delap back on Valentia, where I meet Pam Twentyman, the keeper of Maude Delap's notebooks, in the Heritage Centre. When I arrive, it turns out that I'm sharing my research appointment with another young woman also fascinated with the story of the Delaps – Jane Sheehan. A marine biologist from North Kerry, Jane has long light-brown hair and a poised manner. She's carrying out research as part of an eco-museum in which she'll explore Delap's work, and so Pam takes us both through the photos she has, telling us what she knows of Maude Delap and her great lost love.

Jane and I agree to meet for coffee the following morning where, on a picnic table outside the pub on the harbour, we explore our shared interest, and I feel myself slightly awkward and nervously reaching as Jane explains that the eco-museum she's researching for is part of a project aimed at enabling coastal communities to create opportunities for sustainable tourism. She's gathering and sharing knowledge about Maude Delap because she sees her as such an important figure as regards the heritage of the Iveragh peninsula. A scientist herself, Jane's able to calmly talk me through Delap's scientific work. In 1928, Jane tells me, Delap had been bestowed with a great honour. A sea anemone, *Edwardsia delapiae*, which she had first recorded in eelgrass on Valentia Island's shores, was named after her. A long white wormlike creature with sixteen long translucent tentacles, it is unique to Valentia, an extraordinary-looking animal from the photographs Jane shows me on her laptop, before moving onto pictures of planktons – jellyfish and anemones – the fascinating under-water world Maude Delap sought to capture in her bell jars. Even with the most powerful dark field microscopes in use in research laboratories today, it's hard to see the details that Maude Delap reports in her papers, Jane tells me. 'I'm astonished,' she says, 'at how she managed to get such detailed information considering her equipment.'

Jane suspects that Delap used formalin at 5 per cent in seawater as a preservative for the bell jar speci-mens that she sent to the museum. Formalin is a kind of embalming fluid still used today and it's carcinogenic. You can make it yourself, Jane says, but it's more likely that Delap got it from the hospital on the island. In a twenty-first-century laboratory, whenever a specimen is taken out of preservation to look at, scientists use a fume hood to remove toxic matter from the formalin before they look at it under a microscope. But there were no fume hoods in Delap's day and it's unlikely that she used a mask. Despite this, Maude Delap outlived all of her sisters, dying in July 1953 at the great age of eighty-six. The decomposing specimens that were leftover in 'The Department' were taken out of her house in a wheelbar-row and dumped in a deep pit near where she'd once buried the True's beaked whale.

It makes me sad think of her laboratory emptied like this – the toxic evidence of her unstoppable curious nature turned out into the soil. This woman who had learnt on the job, but had nevertheless made her own laboratory to achieve scientific firsts. Although they were very different scientists with different preoccupations, Maude Delap's story has further overturned my assumptions about what life was for the women of the past on these Atlantic edgelands. The scientific community across Ireland and Britain to which Ellen Hutchins had been connected was by Maude Delap's time, a century later, even more professionalised. Although Delap was unable to go to Plymouth to take up the job she was offered, she was still offered it – something that would have been unheard of in previous eras. Delap's story shows how the path of women was slowly progressing towards the independence I enjoy today.

As I leave the island that afternoon, I contemplate whether telling the story of Maude Delap's supposed great unrequited love takes away from her scientific achievements, which, after all, are what she should be remembered for. But in fact, the more I have learnt about her enthusiasm, her clear passion for life, the more this element of her character has endeared her to me. Maude, if the stories are true, believed in romantic love and really did want a companion. She wore her heart on her sleeve even though the object of her affections did not return them. This is surely something almost everyone can identify with – fancying someone who couldn't care less. It's her steadfastness, her sincerity in the story of her misguided quest for the impossible that has made her come alive to me, made me begin to think of her, as the islanders obviously did, very fondly. It reveals her character in a way I can relate to, without somehow taking away from her achievements. It is a reminder to me of how complicated, how multi-faceted people are. How great achievement can live alongside human foibles and unspoken longings. Perhaps this more sympathetic, more rounded approach to character is something I need to remember next time I find myself criticising or judging myself for my own life choices.

4. BIG PEIG

Peig Sayers
The Great Blasket Island, County Kerry

On the coast road past Caherdaniel, I turn back on myself, looping around the Iveragh penin-sula to stop for the night with relatives – my mother's first cousin Con and his wife, Monica. They live on the road between Sneem and Kenmare, not too far from Blackwater Bridge, where my great-grandparents Ellen and John Cotter ended up when they eventually left Cape Clear Island in 1920. It is a visit my mother has encour-aged – she and Con spent summers together playing here when she was a child and she has fond memories of him and of Blackwater itself.

I feel oddly nervous – I've never met Con and Monica. To which my mother replies that of course I've met them – weren't they at my christening? The visiting of relatives has become a regular point of discussion in our phone con-versations as I head up the coast, and I feel guilty about not stopping in to see everyone. I had meant to, but it's become obvious that it just won't be possible, what with the amount of planning, reading and walking I've set out to do. Heading out from Kenmare, I struggle to find Con and Monica's house in the end, driving up and down the lane until I remember that I have an Eircode and nose the car into what I hope is the right drive.

In the end I needn't have worried. They're delighted to see me and I'm very taken by their house, which truly has the greatest kitchen window view I have ever seen. 'We wondered if you'd make it,' Monica teases, before telling me I have my dad's laugh. I hand her a pear and almond tart I've bought in a bakery on the way, and it's the ultimate faux pas – Monica's made her own apple tart. After dinner she asks which I'd prefer, as if there could ever be a contest, and when I'm fed, Con takes me down to Blackwater Bridge and the house my great-grandparents used to live in.

The house, perched on the side of the river, is a work of art from the turn of the century with a garden and yew tree towering over it. It has thin arched windows with leaded panels and a gable, with a lantern hanging above the doorway. The journey the Cotters took here in 1920 was by boat, from Cape Clear's South Harbour up the coastline, and Con tells me that, despite his intricate knowledge of the Irish coast, the story goes that John somehow missed Blackwater Pier on the way up and continued into Kenmare Bay, only realising the mistake when the mast hit the Kenmare suspension bridge – I can only imagine Ellen tight-lipped as they struggled to repair it.

Ellen Cotter was my own age when they decided to move from Cape Clear, and the tides of time were working against the islanders. Lace was now made by machines and so could no longer feed families; oceans were beginning to be deep-water trawled on an industrial scale, and local fishermen just couldn't compete. Here in Blackwater Bridge, for the next few decades, the Cotters ran the local post office from this quaint two-storey cottage. They had bought it from an engineer and architect called George Lucid, who lived here with his wife – yet another Ellen, Ellen O'Sullivan – and child in the 1890s and died as a widower in February 1912. Con was told as a child that George Lucid took stone left over from the nearby Parknasilla Hotel to build the wall outside the house, so it is entirely possible that Lucid built the house itself too.

Ellen Cotter had two more babies here, adding to the seven surviving children they already had, while my great-grandfather took up writing poetry as a hobby. His poems are lyrical romantic verses, a little like songs, often about his life as a fisherman on Cape Clear, and he also wrote one about Con himself, who served in Cyprus with the Irish army as a United Nations peacekeeper. I don't know whether Ellen Cotter continued to make lace, but as far as I know, none of her work survives. I find it hard to imagine she didn't, given my own mother's and aunt's incredible knitting and crochet capacities.

Con remembers Ellen Cotter in her seventies – confined to bed and unable to straighten her legs. 'She was good to me, anyway,' he says, before telling me she used to give him half a crown from her pension every Friday. I'm pleased to hear that she had this generosity of spirit – it is the only direct memory of her that I have gathered. As we peer over Blackwater Bridge at what must be a fifty-metre drop, Con tells me he used to walk along the top of it as a child. One time his grandfather saw him, he says, and simply raised his eyebrows and looked away. Perhaps he thought a bit of danger was healthy, I surmise. 'Maybe so, but when you think of the amount of children that would have been around here, I don't how any of us never fell in,' he says. On this summer evening, tragedy seems a long way away and Blackwater Bridge a happy place.

The Cotters were ahead of the curve in leaving Cape Clear, although most young islanders would travel much further than Kerry. By 1936, as Éamon Lankford notes in his island history, almost half of Cape Clear Island's once six-hundred-strong population had emigrated. A type of island existence was ending, a way of life that can really only be understood through the words of one woman: Irish oral storyteller Peig Sayers. Born in 1873, just seven years before my great-grandmother, the record she left behind of her life in this period, I am hoping, might mirror some of Ellen Cotter's experience and fill in the gaps for me about everyday life for island women at this time.

*

It's another hot July day, as I sit on the pier at Dunquin. There's a black tarred currach overturned behind me, and I wait for the ferry that will take me out to An Blascaod Mór – the Great Blasket Island. The sea is, in the words of Peig Sayers, 'as calm as new milk', the sun bright in a cloudless sky for the sailing. As we near the island, I follow Wolfie, the skipper's dog, hopping from the small ferry onto the dinghy that'll take us into the

Great Blasket pier. Once landed, I slowly trek up the stone steps onto the road of the dead and into the centre of the island. The road is called this, I'll later learn, because there was no cemetery on the island so this was the road by which, eventually, every inhabitant would leave to be buried on the mainland.

The Great Blasket Island has been uninhabited since 1953, but at the top of this steep hill there's now a café for day trippers alongside the few remaining cottages in which visitors like myself can delight in what is now marketed as rustic charm. A couple of donkeys with shaggy hair loiter outside the café, staffed by Lesley Kehoe, who tells me how she fell in love with the island by studying the literature of the Great Blasket as part of her master's thesis. She and her partner, Gordon, are, for this summer, the caretakers of the island. Lesley checks the booking diary to see which cottage I'm staying in and has a moment of doubt. 'Is this right?' she asks someone at the back of the shop. A muttering confirms that it is. I can't believe my good fortune. I'm staying the night in Peig Sayers's house.

Lesley leads me across to the two-storey cottage that was Peig's home from her mid-thirties, in 1910 until 1942, when she returned to the mainland and her birthplace of Dunquin. As Irish language and culture was reborn against the background of the fight for Irish independence, scholars and folklorists flocked to this house on a tiny Atlantic island to visit a woman they'd heard had the ancient gift of Irish storytelling. Peig was an oral storyteller – a *seanchaí*. In a world before radio or television, her great skill was the ability to hear and recall tales that had been passed down through generations, and she became a huge resource of Irish folklore. From

Peig alone, folklorist W. R. Rodgers records in his introduction to *An Old Woman's Reflections*, the Irish scholar
Seósamh Ó Dálaigh collected 375 tales. Memory was at
the heart of the Irish oral culture that had survived on this
island despite centuries of British colonisation. Here on
the Great Blasket, Peig's stories were preserved against all
odds, just at the moment before modernity took over and
a way of life was lost forever.

Her autobiography, *Peig*, a later book of folk tales
and memories, *An Old Woman's Reflections*, as well
as two more recent collections of her stories give an
unparalleled insight into the life of an Atlantic island
woman – the first to tell the tale of her life in the Irish
language. In becoming known as a storyteller, Peig had
forged a unique path. Kerry tradition supposedly had it
that the gift of poetry passed from father to daughter,
while the gift of story – of Irish heroes and popular folk
tales – passed from father to son. But as W. R. Rodgers
again recalls, Peig defied this, learning stories from her
father as a child when they went *ag bothántaíocht* – on
nightly visits to the neighbours. Peig could recite from
memory many of the longer folk tales.

Peig Sayers is the most famous of a crop of great writers who lived together on this island community in the
1920s and 1930s, which was then part of the Gaeltacht
– the districts of Ireland where Irish is the first language. Alongside her lived Tomás Ó Criomhthain, who
wrote *The Islandman*, Muiris Ó Súilleabháin, author of
Twenty Years a-Growing, and Eibhlís Ní Shúilleabháin,
whose writing has been collected in *Letters from the
Great Blasket*. Read together with Peig's work, these
books provide a picture of Gaeltacht community life

here on the fringes of Europe. But unlike her peers, Peig's words were not written down by her own hand but by her son Mícheál or by other scholars who came to visit, as Peig herself could not read or write her own first language of Irish, having received her early education in English.

The good weather is holding up, the temperature nearing the mid-twenties, but inside Peig's stone house it's cool and airy. Lesley and I have somehow caught an air of mischief – we joke that an old blanket in the main room is Peig's distinctive shawl, the one she's wearing in every photograph ever taken of her. It makes her instantly recognisable and, it must be said, doesn't help her evade parody. Because ever since Peig's autobiography was first published in 1936, she's battled with a stereotype – that she's a miserable old widow who moans relentlessly about her lot. Her very name seems to bring an almost involuntary eye roll to most of my Irish friends, often along with a few swear words. 'Peig, that old bitch', one said they used to call her. A quick web search shows that some newspaper articles even call her 'the most hated woman in Irish history'. Her unforgivable crime seems to be that her autobiography was part of the compulsory Irish school-leaver's curriculum – a painful experience that extended across several generations.

Obviously, since I was born and grew up in Britain, my view of Big Peig, or Peig Mhór, as the islanders called her, is untouched by learning Irish. Despite being warned that I'd find Peig both dour and sanctimonious, when I read her collection of stories, *An Old Woman's Reflections*, in translation of course, I was surprised at how much I enjoyed her. Now, here I stand with Lesley, leaning across Peig's white-painted half-door, as the stream of day trippers who came on the ferries passes by on the narrow track from the harbour.

'Keep this door closed until the last ferry goes,' Lesley tells me. 'People will try to come in thinking the house is a museum otherwise.'

We look out at the view of the Blasket Sound, an often-treacherous stretch of sea between here and the mainland where Peig was born. Not an hour ago I was sitting there, on the Dunquin Harbour steps.

'One thing about Peig,' says Lesley, 'people might think she moaned a lot, but she had a great view.'

For generations, Peig's moaning was openly ridiculed in Ireland, most famously by Flann O'Brien in *An Béal Bocht* or *The Poor Mouth*, which satirises the relentless hardship of her Blasket memoir. I'm only halfway through Peig's autobiography, but so far, with its tales of cake pilfering and blind man's buff, I'm finding it quite joyful. I tell Lesley that it reminds me in some ways of Laurie Lee's *Cider with Rosie*.

'The early days are the best,' says Lesley, nodding.

'Does it get worse?'

'It does, but look,' she says, 'although she has this reputation for being miserable, by all accounts from people who knew her Peig was great craic.'

Months later, having sought out these accounts recorded by other islanders and scholars of the time, such as W. R. Rodgers, Robin Flower, Seosamh Ó Dálaigh, Kenneth Jackson, Máire Ní Ghuithín and others, I discovered that Peig's house was a social centre of the Great Blasket – where the young people of the island gathered nightly to hear her stories. That, despite her admittedly often mournful tone in *Peig*, there are many reports of her racy language and charming, even flirtatious manner towards the endless flock of young British and Irish scholars who came to visit. In Robert Kanigel's *On an Irish Island*, he tells the story of Celtic linguist Kenneth Jackson, an English man educated at Cambridge, spent the summers from 1932 to 1937 on the island gathering Peig's stories. When he first came to the Blaskets, wearing shorts, knee socks and a brass buckled belt, he was just twenty-three years old and Peig was fifty-eight. At first, Kanigel tells, Jackson spoke no Irish and so took down Peig's tales with a phonetic alphabet, which he would then read back for her to correct. He had no idea, at first, what the words meant, but she would correct any mistakes and then explain each story to him in English too. Jackson described Peig as tall with violet eyes and blonde hair, a person who was shrewd but fun. He says that he became devoted to her. That he almost fell in love with her.

Lesley leaves me to settle in and I take a proper look around the house. There's no hot water or electricity on the island so the little galley kitchen is spartan – just a hob and some cupboards full of half-empty bags of cereal, plastic forks and packets of salt left over from previous guests. On the other side of the room is a fireplace – Peig's fireplace – complete with iron poker, around which it's easy to conjure up a sense of the past. In her memoir *While Green Grass Grows*, folklorist Bríd Mahon told how Peig, even in her seventies, could switch on her magnetic personality – a man's woman who would flirt with the male visitors as they came to take their seats around the fire, offering them each a drop of whiskey.

Above the fireplace hangs an ingenious wooden clothes rack that can be lowered and lifted as necessary, and in the centre of the room, a fake leather three-piece sofa that looks like it arrived here sometime in the 1990s. A Welsh dresser holds a series of framed black and white photos of former islanders. In the first photograph, four flat-capped men dig foundations, while a man with a straw hat and tie looks on; in the next, a class and their schoolmistress stand outside a schoolhouse, the image so old that their faces are just pale blurs looking out from the past. The last picture shows Peig Sayers in late middle age sitting outside what must be this house. She's wearing her woollen shawl and a gingham skirt and smiling broadly. While I've been idling around the front room, Lesley's been replaced by my housemates for the weekend – a couple from Dublin who I think are on a romantic weekend of freedom; they've just dropped a child off at Cork university and I sense some awkwardness at my presence. I decide, while the weather is still good, to give them some space for the evening and so, rucksack packed, I set out to walk the island.

The Great Blasket Island is long and narrow – six kilometres long by one kilometre wide, with a hill down the centre of its northern half. Peig describes it as 'shaped like a whale sleeping on the surface of the calm ocean'. My walk will take me in a loop around the whale's tail fins and body, making up the east part of the island, and then west over to its upper body of Croughmore, the island's highest point. Beyond this, I hope to walk over the island's westernmost tip and then finally back around the other side in a loop. It should take me four or five hours, into the evening. Away from the house, the upper road leads me north-east, through the remains of the old nineteenth-century village perched overlooking the tiny harbour. Here, dug into the hillside that faces the mainland, are the houses of Peig's fellow writers Tomás Ó Criomhthain and Muiris Ó Súilleabháin. And here, of course, is Peig's first house, the one she lived in before 1910, now crumbling but still mainly intact. These houses were built to last – the thick, drystone walls so resistant to decay that I can still see the exact layout of the rooms. It's hard to believe it could ever contain the at least ten children that Peig had with her husband, Pádraig, of whom only six survived.

Seeing the houses lying abandoned all together like this, huddled in on top of each other, I feel witness to the remnants of an old, almost medieval way of life in which privacy was unheard of. People must have known almost everything about each other in this isolated community – from their bowel movements to the states of their marriages, not to mention being kept awake by crying babies and overtired children. Peig's stories often centre around how community life goes awry. Men scorned complain of the treachery of women; rivals argue over hens in Dunquin; drink is the ruin of many a man and a good match is everything. In Peig's world, I realise as I read, a mean or lazy husband would be the worst fate of all. Perhaps that is still true today.

Like my great-grandmother on Cape Clear, Peig was an outsider from the mainland who entered the community through marriage to a fisherman. But unlike Ellen Cotter, who had already started an independent adult life by training as a lacemaker, Peig had limited options. After five years in domestic service in Dingle, she was matched, at the age of nineteen, by her brother and father to an islandman, Pádraig Ó Guithín, twelve years her senior. She tells that her affection for her brother Seán was so high that if he had ordered her to go and bail the ocean, she would have done so. She watched as her father drank and spoke with three men, one of whom she knew she'd be marrying. 'I didn't open my mouth, but I was peeping from under my eyelashes at the young men because I knew none of them and I could neither choose one nor bar any.' On 13 February 1892 she moved to this thousand-acre island – the 'lonely airy place' she had so often stared at from her childhood home in Dunquin. She would later tell the folklorist W. R. Rodgers that it had been a love match, so presumably she quickly grew to love her husband once he had been selected for her.

Up the rising track I climb, past the island's water tank that someone – perhaps missing a draught pint – has painted to look like a glass of Guinness, where the main road leads me in a loop around a large bare hillside on the north-east of the island. Here the grass is rough and shaggy, with pink flowering heather scattered across it. This hill forms the central spine of the whale shape that Peig describes and is without a single tree. From this side of the island, I can see the mainland of the Dingle Peninsula in front of me and look upon my past travels – Beara, Iveragh and the Skelligs in the distance.

The first hour is easy walking, but slowly it becomes steeper and steeper. Whales and dolphins are often seen on this stretch of water but today I see only a flat blue line. Falling beneath the path lie the green fields of the Great Blasket, the ridges on which the islanders once grew potatoes. Wherever I am, I feel the danger of a rolling drop down across these fields into the ocean. The sea was central to life on the island, and from Peig's words I can conjure the excitement across the community when mackerel shoaled on the surface of the water; her utter dread of her husband not returning from fishing trips; her anger and fright spilling over as she tries to keep her children from running out to the cliff edge. 'The breed of the sea was in them,' she says. 'Often I'd smash their toy boats.' These volatile waters dictated the significant moments in Peig's and the other islanders' lives – from baptism at a few days old to the moment they were carried off to be buried on the mainland. The islanders who didn't emigrate rarely moved from the island and had a name for every field and cove, a profound affinity with this Atlantic landscape that is now lost.

I stop to rest for a while, fascinated by the different colours that mark the ocean between here and the Beara Peninsula – great patches of indigo cut across by lighter lines where depth or algae alter the shade. The ocean bed around the Great Blasket is uneven and the tidal streams are strong. Here on a sunny Sunday afternoon in July, it's easy to understand Peig's affection for this place. 'It was a lovely night,' she tells us in *An Old Woman's Reflections* of a night-time trip from Dingle, 'the air was clean, full of brilliant stars and the moon shining on the sea. From time to time a sea-bird would give a cry. Inside the black caves where the moon was not shining the seals were lamenting to themselves. I would hear, too, the murmuring of the sea running in and out through the clefts of the stones and the music of the oars cleaving the sea across to Ventry.'

The trek becomes harder as I approach the site of An Dún, where an Iron Age ring fort once stood around 800 BCE, the first known settlers on this isolated place. I climb over the island's first hill, Slievedonagh, and then to its highest point of Croaghmore. Peig describes shivering with dread as she walked here on her first day on the island as a newly married woman, back in 1892. The path is now extremely narrow and precipitous, with a sheer drop down the cliffs at either side, and I have to sit down until my own skin stops crawling from the vertigo. If the looped track I've just trodden was along one side of the island's spine, I've now reached the whale's delicate upper vertebrae, beyond which lies its rarely visited head. On either side of me, flat stones stick out from the side of the cliffs, creating precarious platforms over the sea, like a row of jagged teeth.

My trail notes become jittery. Although the track continues to the very end of the island, most walkers turn back here, they read. But months later, reading *Peig* again, I wonder to myself if this next part of the island is where the islanders used to cut the turf in winter and where in 1920 – the year my great-grandparents were sailing to Kenmare – Peig's second-youngest son, Tomás, fell from the cliff and died. He was around fourteen years old. Turf was scarce that year and so Tomás had been gathering heather from the hillside to burn on the fire when he slipped. Eight men in two currachs had gone out to bring back the body, and Peig describes how, instead of in the ocean, they had found him laid out on a flat piece of stone like a table, the sea moving around him. In later life, Peig often told the tale of how, when Tomás's teenage body was brought home, his head had hit the rocks so hard that he couldn't be presented for his wake. She had used her hands to massage his skull back into shape and then wash and clean him. Peig had already lost three of her ten children at birth and a little girl, Siobhán, who was just eight when she died from measles. It is hard to begrudge her her sorrow.

The joy of *Peig* is in this honesty – this complete account of what life was like. There are moments where she feels overly pious, and I can see that an older woman mourning her sorrows wasn't the right person for teenagers full of hope and possibility to learn Irish from. But for me, reading in translation, it is full of moments of delight. Peig spares no one – not even herself – in her tales of how everyday life was lived for this generation of women. From the day teenage Peig, a maid herself, belts a cocky houseboy with a rotten turnip, to scraps over men in milkhouses and drunken days at the races, Peig tells it how it is. In her world, women say what they think and give as good as they get. One of my favourite moments in her collection *An Old Woman's Reflection*s is when she refuses to give up her seat on the train in Dingle to an English-speaking gentleman, as she has the same right to it as him.

The abilities that Peig herself possessed in abundance – to hold your own in conversation, verbally assert yourself and tell a good story – are considered by her to be the ultimate mark of character: a quality as highly esteemed as generosity towards one's neighbours. This esteem for the value of speech is the thing I have taken most from Peig Sayers and her work. Growing up, at school and then later at work, people have always remarked on how much I talk. I often try to hold back, feeling that I'm taking up more than my share of airtime, trying not to dominate. Travelling here in Ireland, I'm unexpectedly feeling completely at home in this element of my character. People chat to me everywhere – swimming in the sea on Bealtra pier, outside derelict copper mines, in the grocer's shop at Annascaul, from the car in the middle of the road – and nobody has commented that I talk too much. It's just part of the flow of everyday life on this shoreline.

It is freeing – I feel relief from a constant everyday bind that I was only partly aware of. And it's a pleasure to be met in conversation with time and interest. Travelling alone, I'm also beginning to realise that when people talk to me, they are more open. It's if by being alone, by passing through, I'm allowing them to reveal themselves – a whole person, apart from their partners or children. It's made me think more about life in small communities, versus the big city anonymity I am used to. How much did Peig have to perform a role to fit into this small community? She was both completely known as a big personality yet also might have had to present herself as a pious widow to fit in. Did she create a persona that still follows her about to this day?

Climbing up the narrow track, I struggle on until before me lie the green fields that lead to the tip of the island. I make my way slowly down towards it, past an old stone sheep dip and the grassy, bumpy outline of what looks like another Iron Age enclosure, until I can go no further. This is An Ceann Dubh, the Black Head of the island. I sit down on the long grass and look out at the tiny western Blaskets – Inishnabro and Inishvickillane. Today these westerly islands are veiled in a white haze so that they seem like apparitions, as if they couldn't possibly be real. I'm exhausted, exhilarated and in awe of the islanders' physical fitness. Just to pick potatoes from these fields would have required a stamina I do not possess. No wonder Peig lived until she was eighty-five years old.

Alone on this cliff, I feel a sense of unexpected stillness. A sense that I am in myself, complete. Sitting here, with no other thought or concern of another person or any other place, I have the sensation of being not only remote physically from my normal life, or indeed any life at all, but also of having entered a new part of time – a place frozen, where nothing has changed for millennia. Months later, re-reading *An Old Woman's Reflections*, I am recalled to this moment of peace that I experienced, as Peig describes sitting on the cliff bank in the days after having buried one of her children.

> I sat on the bank above the beach where I had a splendid view all around me. Dead indeed is the heart from which the balmy air of the sea cannot banish sorrow and grief.

Taken by the view, Peig puts down the stocking she is knitting.

> The whole bay was calm as new milk, with little silver spray shimmering on its surface under a sunlight that was then brilliant. To the south Slea Head stood boldly in view as if it would stand there forever.

The island has this effect. Of being part of time passing. Sitting there, mourning the death of her children, inviting nature to somehow ease her pain, she tells a neighbour, Seán Eoghain, that she can see Hy-Brasil, the enchanted island that the islanders believed would appear once every seven years. He replies, with kindness and brusque common sense, that it's time for her to stop dreaming and be off home.

I turn, regretfully, back towards Croaghmore. It's past six now and in this evening heat the insect life of the island is in a frenzy. Huge beetles cross my path, tiny white moths circle the path edge, and meadow-brown butterflies emerge from the grass. On the shoreline beneath me the rocks around the island are covered in gulls. Walking onto the main looped track, I meet Ally McKenzie, a Canadian hitchhiker who came over on the boat with me this morning. She's travelling for a few weeks before going to a friend's wedding in Waterford. Ally's a real backpacker – hitching lifts across Ireland and camping in fields with her one-person tent as she goes. Not like me with my car and my soft city ways. She asks where I'm staying and I tell her about Peig Sayers's house.

'This woman, what's she called? Peig? I had never heard of her before I got here and now she's all anyone wants to talk to me about.' Someone on the boat over has lent Ally a copy of Peig's autobiography and she's been reading snippets of it as she goes.

'I like it,' she says, 'but there's a lot of God.' I tell her what I've learnt so far about Peig's life, about the children she lost. 'That makes sense then,' Ally replies and we have a moment of looking down onto the drop of the cliffs together, of wonder that people ever lived here.

*

Ally comes to the house later that evening, at half eight. It's still light as we head down to the beach – An Trá Bán: the White Strand. The day trippers have gone and left behind are just the caretakers and the ten people camping or staying in the cottages. For the first time I feel how inaccessible, how uninhabited a place this is. Far more remote than Cape Clear or Valentia, where there are still people – pubs, shops and doctors at least. Apart from a couple who are camping and sitting far on the other side, the beach is empty. We hesitate for a moment, contemplating whether to join the grey seals bobbing up and down as they watch us from the water. There are seven of them; their round black heads vanish and then reappear every few seconds. One inquisitive animal comes closer to us with every dive, until he's just about ten metres from the shore. The closest I've ever been before this was watching dappled harbour seals through binoculars from Rainham Marshes back home, where they bask on the banks of the Thames.

Ally's packed so light she has no swimming costume so just strips down to her underwear, while I'm in such a hurry to get in after my long walk that I almost strip naked in front of her. She creases up laughing at me, with the joy of someone with nowhere to go and nothing to do. 'You really want to get in, don't you?' I really do, but it's cold. Ice cold, more so than any water I've yet been in, colder even than Ballydonegan Beach in Allihies. I swim out, the sea floor disappearing beneath me, careful to keep my distance from our curious onlooker. Behind me, Ally is having trouble acclimatising and decides to bail out before she gets any colder. Drying in the sun, we both agree that she did the right thing – the Great Blasket is not the place to get hypothermia.

As Ally heads off for the night to her tent on the hill-side, I return to Tigh Peig, the name of the house, which I have only just realised is written on a slate by the front door. My housemates are out walking, so I decide to make myself tea. As the kettle boils, in the fading light from the window, I notice a *súgán* chair – an extraordinary piece of craftsmanship that I've never encountered before, the straw back and seat intricately woven. It's easy as the sun sets to imagine Peig here sitting by the fire, talking late into the night, entertaining the neighbours with her stories. I gather candles from around the house and head upstairs to my bedroom, where the furniture is minimal – my single bed, another stripped double, an old desk with varnish lifting from its surface and a mirror spotted with age, the dark-teal painted frame cracked and held together with masking tape. A picture of Peig hangs above my bed in the corner, looming over me, and I wonder if any of this might have once been her furniture.

I settle in to read her tales of dancing children, ghosts and cures all originally told in a language that I cannot access, that Peig calls 'the language of superior men'. Is it my distance, physically and generationally, from Peig Sayers, I wonder, that allows me to enjoy her so much? She does complain about her poverty, but that seems an honest and valid complaint. It was easy to romanticise life on this island and on Cape Clear before I had vis-ited, but now I think of carrying sacks of oats or spuds along that rocky path in the rain or having to face the neighbours when your child is in her last hours.

Peig wasn't always old and dressed in a black shawl. There is young Peig, angry and giving out to the houseboy, determined teenage Peig deciding she might as well make a match. Laughing middle-aged Peig, flirting with folklorists Kenneth Jackson or Robin Flower because, well, why not – they're hanging on her every word anyway. I think about this woman whose mind held hundreds of folk tales and verses she had picked up throughout her life and wonder how much of her piety, her stance of being an old wise woman, was a persona and how much was her true essence. There are still five thousand pages of oral material collected from Peig in the archives of University College Dublin, much of which has not been published or translated into English. W. R. Rodgers described her as a light-hearted woman, who in performance could change her mood and facial expressions quickly. She would use her hands deftly to tell her tales – clapping at important moments or raising her hand to her lips to disclose secrets. She was a performer as well as a storyteller – were she alive today, I think she would have become an actress. It's clear to me that much of the delight of Peig's stories is lost in reading them rather than watching her perform.

Peig had spirit. Defying every expectation of a woman of her class and occupation, her story has survived, and it is deeply wedded to both this landscape and the Irish culture that she celebrates. It's true she has a maudlin edge, formed by living for many decades on the edge of life and death, but she's made me realise that I hadn't fully appreciated how hard life was for my ancestors living here along this shoreline. She's so honest about her hardships that, when reading, I sometimes felt uncomfortable and upset too. Peig's words are confronting, in a way, because it's difficult for me to imagine a world in which my options are as limited as Peig's were. But at the end of it all, her great gift as a storyteller triumphs – Peig had the last laugh. There is no more famous autobiography in Ireland, and despite a life in the service of others – first as a maid and then as a mother – she is remembered as completely her own person. Known by her first name, she owns her identity completely.

Peig has made me think more deeply about storytelling. About whose stories survive. As I travel, I haven't told everyone I meet about this intent of my journey – about the women I am following and how I am writing as I go. But the stroke of fortune that meant I ended up sleeping in one of Peig's bedrooms has made me feel that I am on the right path. As Lesley showed me around yesterday morning, I had felt able to confide in her about my book – about the research and walks I had already done and those I was planning to do. Lesley had been attentive and unhesitatingly supportive. 'These women's stories are important,' she'd said, and I had felt lifted and more confident in a way I hadn't before. It was a feeling that stayed with me as I walked this island.

I contemplate this new feeling as my Sunday begins with a shockingly cold shower, washing the salt from last night's swim off my skin. My plan for today is to head to Limerick, to my Aunt Jean's house, from where I hope to walk over the next couple of days along the River Shannon, looking for the house where the late-nineteenth-century nationalist and campaigner Charlotte Grace O'Brien once lived.

After another calm crossing to the mainland, Ally and I together climb the perpendicular footpath of Dunquin Harbour where, out of breath at the top, we exchange addresses in the way that passing travellers do. I offer her a lift, but she says she'd rather walk to Dingle, and so I start out on the clifftop road along the Slea Head Loop. Two cars can barely pass each other on these hairpin bends, the cliff face on one side and a drop on the other, yet coaches from Killarney block the way at each turn. At one point we are so piled up and I have failed at reversing so many times that one of the coach drivers has to get out and reverse my car himself, so that it is flush to the cliff, while a coach-load of American tourists watch. It is a humbling experience.

The drive from Dunquin to Limerick should only take me two hours but now, wrapped up in Peig's life, I can't help stopping along the way, first at her grave and then in Dingle town where I visit Curran's, a time capsule of a bar where Peig spent some of her years in service. It's covered in wall-to-wall shelving full of clutter from its thirties heyday – race-day posters and porter bottles, piles of newspapers and violin cases – along with a resident bunch of local barflies and the occasional bemused tourist. It isn't hard to imagine Peig standing in the doorway here, looking to find out the latest news and plotting her big escape. Because like many young Irish women of the 1880s and 1890s, Peig Sayers hadn't expected to live out her days in Ireland.

The teenage Peig had dreamt of emigration to New York, where her best friend Cáit Boland had gone before her. In the end, Cáit couldn't work due to a hand injury and was unable to send the price of the fare. Having drawn the short straw, Peig weighed up her options and decided that marriage was better than servitude. It must have been a crushing disappointment for her. In 1892, the year she married Pádraig, historian W. D. Griffin records in his book *The Irish in America* that 48,966 people left Ireland for the Port of New York. It was part of a larger pattern that had been established in the most horrific famine years of 1845 to 1852. Although starvation was never again on the scale of those years, bad harvests and political turmoil meant that hunger and the exodus continued. Between 1856 and 1921, 3.6 million emigrants left Ireland for America, and between 1871 and 1951, when Peig was alive, ten women emigrated for every eight men. And as historian Chandra Miller notes, 89 per cent of these women were single and under twenty-four.

Often funding their passage through needlework or knitting, they crossed the Atlantic in search of new lives, on board ocean liners that could carry up to a thousand passengers. The voyage to America lasted just over a week. Campaigner Charlotte Grace O'Brien documented the experiences of these young emigrant women in the late nineteenth century, and it is her story that I intend to explore next. A writer and aristocrat who lived from 1886 on the banks of the River Shannon in Foynes, not far from where my own mother grew up, I'm hoping that her work might help me understand why these women left in such numbers.

5. THE SHIPS

Charlotte Grace O'Brien
Foynes, County Limerick

At the window there's a hooded crow making a noise so primeval that it wakes me from my sleep. It's Monday morning and I'm at my Aunt Jean and Uncle Bill's house in County Limerick. There's an electric blanket on my bed and a digital clock on the bedside cabinet, reading 10.30 a.m. I've been asleep for thirteen hours. 'You're white as a sheet,' my aunt had said when I arrived last night. I'd struggled to keep my eyes open while I ate dinner and had gone to bed straight after, while it was still light. Perhaps, I consider, lying there in the bed, that although I'm finding little to complain about on this journey, the sheer energy I'm expending on so much walking and driving is taking a physical toll.

'The dead awaken,' says my Aunt Jean as I emerge into the kitchen for breakfast, and in truth, I do feel resurrected after my long sleep. I sit eating my cornflakes, contemplating how much nicer the milk is here than it is in London and moving in and out of concentration while Jean and

Bill talk about their grandchildren. Jean is my mother's sister and she and her husband Bill are two of the calmest, kindest people I know. They are anchoring people, whom I have known my whole life and with whom I always feel completely at home. Bill spent his working life as an oyster farmer on the Shannon and so the conversation naturally turns to the coastline. I tell them about the notice I had seen in Bantry. How it protested cutting the kelp forests and how I am starting to think about how we treat the ocean. Bill tells me that he knew climate change was real when he saw Japanese cold water oysters spawning because the temperature in the River Shannon had risen too high.

My Limerick family all live alongside the estuary of this great river that splits Ireland in two. I have vague memories of flying into Shannon airport, of swimming at Ringmoylan when I was a child with my cousins, that I try to recall as I set out from Foynes. My walk today will take me along the Shannon riverbank – a route that the nationalist and campaigner Charlotte Grace O'Brien, a great swimmer herself, writes, in a collection of her work compiled by her nephew, the Irish journalist Stephen Gwynn, that she did in the evenings from her house, Ardanoir. Mid-morning, having been told by Jean and Bill that there's parking by the harbour, I follow signs to Foynes Port and drive into a world of pipes and cables, shipping containers and temporary offices for companies I've never heard of – Argonaut and Inver and Atlantic Fuel Supply. From the signs on the backs of the lorries, this is what seems to come in and out of the port of Foynes: oil, coal and chemicals; cement, construction materials and animal feed.

I watch a crane scoop a green substance from one container and deposit it into another. At first I think it might be some kind of soil but soon I realise it's gravel being poured like water. A neon-clad driver coming the opposite way in his forklift gives me a curious look, and I realise that I've somehow wandered into a male world where I don't belong. At the end of the road, a sign warns of restricted access and so I drive back through barriers I perhaps should never have entered and make my way back to the main street of Foynes, where I park up outside the chemist and change into my walking boots.

There's an air of sleepiness in Foynes on this hot summer's day. I pass an old storefront with a display of lifebuoys in the window; a pub – The Shannon Bar – upon the wall of which are painted the fading words 'Roaring Megs'; and finally the museum dedicated to the flying boats that once took off and landed in the Shannon throughout the 1930s. Just outside the town, a single red cargo ship lies in the harbour, across from which lies Foynes Island – which my uncle and aunt call O'Brien's Island. All of this land, including the woodland that fringes the estuary, was once part of the O'Brien family's 6,500-acre Monteagle Estate. Charlotte Grace O'Brien grew up at one of their big houses – Cahermoyle, just 15 kilometres from here. Born in 1845, the year that marked the first failure of the Irish potato crop and the start of the Great Hunger, she witnessed throughout her childhood how the tenants on the O'Brien lands emigrated en masse. By the end of this famine, as I read in Tyler Anbinder's epic history of immigrant New York, around 2 million of Ireland's population of 8.4 million had left and an estimated 1 million people had died.

O'Brien, her nephew Gwynn writes in the memoir that accompanied her work, my main source in understanding her life and work as recounted in these pages, was a daughter of the famous nationalist William Smith O'Brien, who was a direct descendant of the medieval High King of Ireland Brian Boru. Although a landowner and rent collector with tenants himself, William put his own interests aside to become a member of the Young Ireland Party that sought Irish independence, hosting their meetings at Cahermoyle before becoming part of their insurrection in 1848. In his last speech in Westminster, he declared, 'it shall be the study of my life to overthrow the dominion of this parliament over Ireland'. As a result, Charlotte Grace O'Brien was just three years old when her father was sentenced to death and transported for life to Van Diemen's land – now Tasmania. She thus grew up with her family's stance as nationalists at the forefront of her mind, but she also lived a life of privilege far beyond any of the women I have yet encountered on this journey.

I pass the wire fence of the yacht club, the shiny white boats docked in rows, until the drop down to the river beneath to the right becomes green and forested. On the opposite side of the main road appears Ardanoir, the house that Charlotte Grace O'Brien built with the inheritance she received on turning twenty-one. Slightly obscured now by the cypress trees planted when it was built, she called it Ard an Óir in Irish, 'the golden height', reflecting its position on a large sloping hill overlooking the Shannon. Through Lady's Gate, steps lead down into Coillte Wood – a small part of the seventeen acres of woodland along the riverbank. I stop on some steps down into the forest where a red peacock butterfly, bright blue eyes on its wings, settles on the ground beside me. A path winds through a forest of beech trees, Scots pines, Douglas firs, sycamores and birches that bend towards the light of the shore, the river getting closer with every turn.

Before she moved to Ardanoir and began to walk these paths, Charlotte Grace O'Brien's adult life had been spent in the service of others, either nursing her father – who was eventually pardoned – through his last days, or at the grand house of Cahermoyle. There, from the age of twenty-three, she had raised her brother Edward's three children after his wife Mary died in 1868. She loved these children – Nelly, Dermod and Lucy – almost to a fault and yet, her nephew wrote, could never let go of the fact that she did not have a husband or children of her own. When her brother Edward remarried and the children left home, at the age of thirty-four Charlotte Grace O'Brien found herself in search of new purpose. Added to this, her hearing, which had always been bad, finally disappeared completely in 1879, leaving her profoundly deaf. This must have been a confusing time, where she was both liberated and deprived of children that surely felt like her own, while also struggling with the loss of her hearing. She might well have allowed herself to become isolated at this time, but rather than feel defeated, she began to forge a new identity as a writer and political activist. This turn to the wider world and engaging with injustice says a great deal about the temerity of her character. The stoicism she showed in this reminds me, too, of Ellen Hutchins's refusal to give into illness. As a writer, it would be a piece of non-fiction, of reportage in fact, that was to make Charlotte Grace O'Brien famous when, in the spring of 1881, she visited her sister-in-law in Cobh, County Cork.

Then called Queenstown, Cobh was the port most southern Irish emigrants left from. It was here that O'Brien first saw the inside of one of the ships to New York when she requested a tour on the *Germanic*, a White Star Line ocean liner docked in the port.

'I, coming from one of the chief emigrating counties of Ireland, had long wished to see for myself under what conditions the voyage was made,' Charlotte wrote that May of her visit to the *Germanic* in the *Pall Mall Gazette* – a piece called 'The Horrors of an Emigrant Ship', beginning with the scene on the dockside:

> The pier was crowded, mostly with young men and women, a few of the latter carrying young children. Each emigrant must bring on board a mattress, tins, and plate. At first, the bustle of departure, in a few instances the farewells, the buying of little pots of shamrock for the love of the old land, and all the coming and going consequent on the moving of luggage, prevented my being able to judge of the individual faces.

O'Brien described the people she met as marked with sorrow, along with poverty. She saw in their faces 'ignorance, weakness and indecision ... a hopeless submission to daily want'. Once she started chatting to people, however, they came more alive. She met a gentle-faced countryman from Limerick, with wife and children, who was gifted emigration tickets for the family from a first cousin. 'Two hearty merry girls from Dublin. Their bright grey eyes were full of hope and laughter', sisters who were going to Iowa. They had paid their own way and seemed to Charlotte full of confidence, while beside them stood 'a young fellow in a brilliant green and gold Land League tie'. It's easy to imagine Peig Sayers and her friend Cáit as part of this crowd, who were mostly young. On the day Charlotte Grace O'Brien visited there was only one old person, a man from Loughrea, among the 400 people on board – a third of steerage capacity. The *Germanic* had set out from Liverpool and its next stop was New York, so it was well below the amount of people the liner could actually hold. But in her piece, O'Brien notes that, although the *Germanic* was designed to carry 1,000 steerage passengers, the previous year it had carried on one voyage 1,775.

By 1881, the transatlantic journey from Cork to New York that had once taken three weeks took between seven and ten days. Spring was often the busiest time, as that was when the winter stores of potatoes were giving out and people tended to decide that it was now or never. On that first visit to the *Germanic*, Charlotte Grace O'Brien saw that the differences between the upper-class passengers and those in steerage were stark. After some insistence, she was shown the appalling conditions in the large dark hold where the single men slept, before visiting the main steerage quarters. She describes these as between two decks, divided in three with large pieces of sailcloth. Here, hundreds of emigrants slept on top of the mattresses they had brought with them, divided from each other only by small strips of canvas, meaning, effectively, there was no privacy.

What Charlotte Grace O'Brien found most scandalous and propelled her forward as a campaigner on behalf of female emigrants was that single women were berthed here with married couples. 'Any man,' she wrote, 'who comes with a woman who is or calls herself his wife sleeps by right in the midst of hundreds of young women, who are compelled to live in his presence day and night: if they remove their clothes it is under his eyes, if they lie down to rest it is beside him. It is a shame even to speak of these things; but to destroy such an evil it is necessary to face it.'

She asks her reader to imagine being seasick in the middle of the night, surrounded by a deck full of equally unwell people; to think of little girls lying among 'dissolute men and abandoned women', of 'the living horror menacing the life, honour and soul of hundreds of thousands of our fellow country-women'. Even if the hearty, merry girls she met from Dublin seem like they would look out for each other, the conditions on board sound genuinely dreadful – overcrowded and undignified. And once they arrived at the Port of New York, women would have been immersed in a world they had no knowledge of – liable to robbery, rape or, as O'Brien makes clear, temptation.

Part of me finds O'Brien's description in the *Pall Mall* a little over the top – but then I think of Peig Sayers, how overwhelmed she was on her first day on the Great Blasket, shivering with fright at the sheer cliff drop. Although, as we know from the incident with the turnip and the houseboy, Peig was well able to handle herself, I can also imagine her, and other women like her, more anxious and more vulnerable than we might like to think on this great journey.

Within days of the publication of Charlotte Grace O'Brien's article, questions were being raised in the British parliament about conditions on board the ships. The government officer O'Brien and her sister-in-law had met in Cobh met her again and took her aboard the steerage sections of ten ships to show her that the immigrant girls' beds were divided from those of the families, although admittedly the canvas steerage arrangement could be moved from voyage to voyage. The accusation labelled at O'Brien in parliament was that she had fallen prey – like many a reporter with a good story before and since – to sensationalism. But writing to a number of young immigrant women for testimony, she had it confirmed that, although the beds were divided, all the men and women were in the same room together. She would later refer to the ships she saw as having been in 'show dress'.

This trail through the woods is one O'Brien must have walked often in the evenings, after a long day of writing campaigning letters at her desk, when she was not undertaking the daring river swims that her friend Mary Spring Rice recalled in Gwynn's memoir. The air is cool here and I begin to smell the river. The path twists downwards to the Shannon until I reach Poultallin Point, on the bank of the estuary. Today the tide is coming in and the rocks are covered in dried heaps of bladderwrack. A sign tells me I might see otters or even bottlenose dolphins, but I find only the greyish green water as it laps against the beach. I hear children behind me, and a girl and boy appear with their mother, excited at the prospect of being near the water. 'Look at this,' the little boy says, 'we could go all the way to the sea.'

Undeterred by criticism, Charlotte Grace O'Brien continued her campaign, which appears to have been as anarchic and unique in character as she herself. Although a Protestant, she championed an idea she'd had of a chapter of Catholic ocean nuns who would watch over the young women as they sailed, lobbying priests in Ireland and America in her belief that emigrants would pay sixpence more for such protection. Having seen the conditions in emigrant boarding houses in Cobh, later that same year of 1881, she opened her own, licensed for 105 lodgers, confident that the public's faith in her father's name meant she could not fail. She spent the next year, 1882, in which she turned thirty-seven, visiting three or four ships a day with a medical officer by her side, often beginning at 6 a.m., while 3,000 emigrants passed through her lodgings.

The following year, she travelled to New York, investigating further the conditions on board the ships first hand and staying in a tenement boarding house on Washington Street to gain insight into 'the fate of the innumerable unprotected girls who were swarming through my own hands in Queenstown'. Soon her relentless campaigning took her across America, appealing to Irish Catholic societies to improve the health and safety standards on board each ship as well as to ease the passage of young women out of New York. O'Brien saw the growing city as a depraved place, where mortality rates in the tenements were high and illiterate young women were easy prey for brothel keepers. She sought to encourage women to move immediately out to the Midwest, where she believed the air was cleaner and vice less prevalent.

She was not alone in seeing New York as somewhere to leave as soon as you'd arrived. Vere Foster's 1855 *Penny Emigrant Guide* also told young women to 'leave the overcrowded cities on the sea coast as soon as possible and go up the country, the further the better.'

Now I am down on the bank of the river itself, the forest to my left and Foynes Island to my right. Caves have formed on the left bank, beside which oak trees grow, much older than those in the forest I have just walked through – oak trees that I am sure O'Brien knew when she walked here, planning the opening of her Irish immigrant mission at 7 Broadway in Lower Manhattan, which would eventually befriend over 60,000 women whose friends or family had not showed up at the port of New York or who found themselves robbed or abandoned.

Charlotte Grace O'Brien made a huge difference to the lives of young women travelling to America at the time. By the end of her campaign there were stewardesses on all ships, and she had succeeded in persuading some of the ocean liners to separate the single women from the men and families into separate enclosed berths. She also made progress with hygiene, as the White Star Line began to provide lavatories with soap, wash bowls and towels. Emigrants still had to bring their own bedding on board, but being able to wash must have made the journey more bearable, as well as ensuring that people were likely to be in better health when they arrived in America. There is much to admire about O'Brien's work as a successful campaigner that she performed while profoundly deaf. She seems to have coped with her loss of hearing so well, in fact, that it is rarely mentioned in accounts.

But in truth, although I admire her determination to improve conditions for these many thousands of young women, as well as her desire to protect the vulnerable from rape and sex work once they arrived in New York, the more I read of her writing, the more her tone began, if I am completely honest, to irritate me. From a twenty-first-century perspective O'Brien's self-appointed role as guardian of these young women's well-being can feel somewhat paternalistic. Her preoccupations reflected the views of her time, however – as historian Hasia R. Diner points out in her book *Erin's Daughters in America*, many in the Irish Catholic Church at that time saw the loss of women to emigration as 'the moral murder of countless virtuous Irish maidens'.

Reading through her letters, tucked up in in Jean's spare bedroom this morning, I saw that O'Brien bemoaned never having wed or had children. At first, I felt sympathetic – after all, I have the same concerns myself. But as I read on – to her essay 'The Feminine Animal', in which she puts forward her belief that men are superior to single women, but not to a mother and child – her words made me angry. The notion that Ellen Hutchins or Maude Delap was inferior to anyone simply because she hadn't married or given birth I found ridiculous. Walking here, I wonder how I have allowed myself to fall into a nineteenth-century trap of thinking that I am somehow less valuable as a person because I haven't taken the route expected of women.

The truth is also that, as well as her achievements as a writer and campaigner, O'Brien *was* regarded by her brother's children as close to a mother and clearly loved her very much. Her nephew Stephen Gwynn describes her as 'large, tolerant, humorous, eccentric, ready to laugh and be laughed at', as well as 'courageous physically and morally beyond all measure'. What she comes across as most of all is led by her emotions, a little scattergun, and indeed, Gwynn goes on to say that her hair was often awry and her writing without 'the gift of delicate finish'. While her account of visiting the *Germanic* is at times a brilliant piece of reportage, she does indeed stray into unsound hyperbole – comparing the conditions of the single men's quarters to the transatlantic slave ships that once left West Africa.

Inspired by O'Brien's work, I became curious about the thoughts and feelings of the young female emigrants she wanted to protect. Months after this walk I would seek out their voices in the letters that they left behind – trying to imagine what a life Peig Sayers might have had if Cáit had sent her that ticket to America. I found that the reports of pandemonium at the Port of New York and terrible seasickness in steerage, of women being groped on deck and lacking privacy were all true. As were the tales of brothel keepers waiting in line at Castle Garden, often disguising themselves as employment agencies, and that women made sure to travel in pairs or groups or with local boys who might take care of them. I found that they couldn't always have each other's backs. Sometimes they were entirely fleeced of their money before they left the port. But what I also found was that, on the whole, their new lives in America agreed with them.

Margaret McCarthy from County Cork wrote to her family from New York in September 1850, with the aim of persuading them to join her. 'Any man or woman without a family are fools that would not venture and come to this plentiful country where no man or woman ever hungered or ever will and you will not be seen naked.' She went on to say how glad she was not to have married some 'loammun' or be in the poor house.

In short, for young women there was nothing to stay in Ireland for. In her work, Hasia R. Diner explains how the Famine had destroyed traditional inheritance customs, meaning that one son was often given all the land while his brothers worked for him, and his sisters were sent out to earn a living in farms or shops. Over time it became increasingly difficult to find either work or a husband – not without a dowry anyway. Because of this, in the 1800s women in Ireland began marrying later than in the rest of Europe, meaning that my great-grandmother's marriage at the age of twenty-nine on Cape Clear was not unusual at all.

This is what Charlotte Grace O'Brien's life has led me to – more of an understanding of what life was actually like for women in the late 1800s and early twentieth century, and also what a huge impact the legacy of Famine emigration had. That it created a kind of chain migration that, once started, became an almost unstoppable flow of people – millions and millions of people, entire generations, over 50 per cent of them women. I was lacking this history, and now that I have learnt it, the relationship between Ireland and America is clicking into place for me – the relationship between Ireland and the rest of the world. Why there are millions of people like me, who maybe aren't as close as I am geographically or generationally but are still part of the same diaspora, all able to claim their Irish passports and claim Ireland as home.

In the late 1800s a day labourer called Patrick McKeown wrote home to his sisters from Philadelphia to say that women could get jobs much easier than men, and that you wouldn't be able to distinguish an Irish girl working in America from a prosperous merchant's wife or daughter. The work the women did – mainly domestic – was hard, but the pay-off was immense. Irish women across the Atlantic not only sent money home to help their relatives pay off debts or improve their circumstances – often encouraging them to emigrate too – but also found a freedom impossible in nineteenth-century rural Ireland. The women who moved to America were dependent on no one and free to save up for their own dowries, or indeed to buy the latest clothes – many letters describe fashions or carriages and say to tell the neighbours how well they are doing.

But my favourite letters are those that defy a guarded, chaste life – that hint of freedom and triumph. A letter from a woman called Mary Hanlon to the campaigner Vere Foster in 1865, now in the Public Records Office of Northern Ireland, reads, 'The man I told you about that asked me to marie him, I did not care for him.' In another letter, held in the Irish Folklore Collection, a Mary Brown writes to her Irish friend that she is sorry for the penance the local priest put upon her and encourages her to come to the country of 'love and liberty', where she herself has a good many beaux.

I bring myself back to reality, to putting one foot in front of the other. Beside me runs the river, glinting bright through the trees. The memory of this beauty, of this walk, I know will sustain me once I am back in London, when I am at my desk over winter. Months later, I'll remember it as I leaf through histories of Irish emigration at the British Library in North London in which these women's words are often recalled. Some of the letters are so moving in the way they speak of dreadful homesickness – of loneliness in a completely new country away from those they loved.

It makes me think about how I miss Ireland when I am in London. Whether the feelings I have of wanting to be on these walks – these visits to West Cork or Kerry or along the Shannon or the lanes of rural Sligo – when I'm back in London can be called homesickness.

My mum and dad always called Ireland 'home' when we were growing up, and as a child it annoyed me. After all, Ireland wasn't my home, East London was! After thirty-five years, they finally moved back in 2001, when I was twenty-two, and because they are here now, over the past two decades I've spent much more time in Sligo. Sometimes I come for a couple of months or more, and these longer visits have allowed me to come to appreciate, much more than I did on summer holidays, the beauty of rural Sligo. It's meant that when I go back to London, I really do miss nature and space and the sea – the pure openness of Sligo – as well as missing my parents. But then, when I spend more than a few months here, as I do periodically and am doing now, I miss London. I miss my friends who, like me, often have parents or grandparents from elsewhere in the world. I miss my work and the tension and urgency and pure joy that comes from so many different cultures and types of people living alongside each other.

It can be jarring. One New Year's week a few years ago, I experienced one of the most memorable walks of my life, along a lane by Lough Arrow in the morning – crows moving with me from one telephone wire to the next and frosted patterns on the leaves along the sides of the lane. By the evening, I was back home in London, bedraggled by my budget flight, walking to a Hackney supermarket in abject drizzle, looking at the chewing gum squashed into the pavement and thinking, *Why on earth did I not stay a bit longer?* But when you're away from somewhere it is, of course, easy to romanticise it – as Irish ballads do, reflecting on the themes of leaving. I grew up hearing, and slightly resenting, these songs every Sunday morning in our suburban terraced house, from tapes that my mum bought from an Irish music stall on Walthamstow Market.

I have to ask myself, walking here in Limerick: what are my deeper motivations for this trip? Is it just about exploring the lives of these women – a way to tie together my passions for history and documentary and travel with spending a bit more time in Ireland as my parents get older? Or am I working out some deeper feeling? Is exploring Ireland on my own terms, outside of family holidays or my parents' life, a way of forging a new, more considered connection? Might I, as a couple I hired a camping pod from in Annascaul asked me, be thinking of making Ireland my home?

I come to a square trough on the riverbank, built here God knows when, beside which a metal pole and nine steps lead up into the forest. This was once someone's mooring, but whoever owned it is long gone. I stop and sit down on the steps. I could continue onward, but I don't know how I would then get back up onto the main road that runs parallel to the river. If I were to keep going it would take me directly out into the sea, and I have a sudden urge to do so, to follow the route of the Shannon to its natural end, just like all those young women wondering where their lives might take them.

6. THE CLIFF EDGE

Edna O'Brien
The Cliffs of Moher, County Clare

I still can't shake my fear of swimming alone, no matter how safe the water seems. At Clahane, a natural tidal pool in County Clare, where the shore has eroded into the shape of a horseshoe, I am cautious about going in. I change slowly on the rocks until I am saved – another woman of about my age swims into my eyeline, appears from the sea. She has exactly my colouring, long dark hair like my own and is wearing an almost identical swimsuit to mine. She shows me the barnacled, rusting ladder on the side of the rock, and as my double packs up, I gingerly get in. It's cold and exhilarating, small waves washing over me, Liscannor Bay in the distance. As I swim out to sea I look back to find her waving from the clifftop and I wave back. For the first time when I get out this summer, my skin tingles.

I crossed the River Shannon yesterday and am on the Burren Way now, about to walk a path once taken by one of my heroines and perhaps Ireland's greatest living writer – Edna O'Brien. In 1976, she was filmed on Clare's Cliffs of Moher by a British television crew, who filmed her walking along the cliff edge. In a documentary that was eventually broadcast by ITV, they captured her from a distance, her long bright-red skirt moving with the wind, revealing her legs. She looks joyful and free, here in Ireland to promote a book – *Mother Ireland*, a non-fiction travelogue in which she sought to capture the Ireland that she knew. In it, Edna O'Brien wrote of how Ireland is, and has been since its earliest writings, gendered a woman – 'a womb, a cave, a cow, a Rosaleen, a sow, a bride, a harlot, and of course the gaunt Hag of Beare'. Sometimes she's a romantic damsel in distress waiting to be rescued, such as Dark Rosaleen; a dispossessed heroine who needs her sons to fight for her, such as Kathleen Ní Houlihan; or an old lamenting woman, ravaged by time, like the Hag of Beara, who looks sadly back upon her youth.

It's a week since, on the Beara Peninsula in Cork, I'd passed the rock formation that makes up the original Hag of Beara – a rock said to be where an ancient goddess, the Cailleach, once sat waiting for the god of the sea. This morning I plan to walk to her sister – another rock formation that looks out at the sea – Hag's Head, the most southerly point of the Cliffs of Moher. Starting in Doolin, I'll trek along the edge of the cliffs, a 14-kilometre hike, to this place where legend has it that an old sea witch called Mal fell in love with the hero Cú Chulainn. In the chase that ensued, the hag was dashed against the rocks and then turned to stone as Cú Chulainn escaped across the sea stacks.

In the documentary footage that I have become so captivated by, and which is now held in the British

Film Institute Archives, Edna O'Brien strolls in soft 16-millimetre film along the iconic cliffs as her voice reads the words she wrote about Ireland portrayed as a woman. It's a scene that uses the landscape to distil the view of Edna O'Brien in the mid-seventies, in both Ireland and Britain, as a romantic and unpredictable women's novelist with an interesting private life. Readings from O'Brien's work are illustrated with typical images of how the rest of the world saw Ireland then – the faces of shy, smiling First Holy Communion girls and women gathered outside a church, all to a soundtrack of traditional Irish music.

Doolin, where I'm starting my walk southwards along the cliffs, is known throughout Ireland as a hub of this traditional music. But today is not a day for music and pints. The sky is white and the weather forecast on my phone grim – rain at 100 per cent all day. As I set out on the track, the wind is high and the sea intimidating – huge waves break around the rocks beneath me. Behind me, to the north, I can see the line of the Clare coastline and my first sight of the Aran Islands – faded and foggy in the distance, a thin ghost of themselves. The part of the cliff that Edna O'Brien walks in the documentary is still several kilometres away, midway through the walk I'm about to undertake. It is next to O'Brien's Tower, an observation tower built by a local landlord, Cornelius O'Brien, in the nineteenth century – either for English tourists or to impress the women he was courting, depending on which story you believe.

Edna O'Brien is over ninety now, but when *Mother Ireland* was published she was forty-five, just a few years older than I am, and living and writing in London as she had done, by that point, for seventeen years. Returning to her home county of Clare, she walked these cliffs that are the ultimate symbol of Ireland – so much so, in fact, that they illustrate the second page of my new Irish passport. Being filmed on the Clare coast was something she had also done the previous year, in a documentary called *My Own Place: Edna O'Brien Comes Back to County Clare*, now available on the RTÉ Archives website, that opened with her on the shore of Lahinch, where her short story 'I Was Happy Here' had been filmed. In the Irish documentary, the voiceover was more cutting – speaking of her description of Ireland as controversial and wounding and describing her as, in other people's eyes, 'a scarlet woman'.

Edna O'Brien's reputation had been formed by her first novel, *The Country Girls*. Inspired by her own childhood here in rural Clare, when it appeared in 1960 it created shockwaves throughout Ireland. It is a spirited masterpiece – a visceral and honest book, full of life and youth. It tells the story of two teenage girls from Limerick who are desperate to escape convent-school life for the big city. And escape it they do – to a Dublin of dances, romance and liquor and even adultery through chance and planned encounters. Their restless youthful appetites rejected completely the power structures of 1950s rural Ireland – of fathers, family shame and the Church. The book flew off the shelves.

I make my way along the ridge of the exposed cliff faces, where countless notices warn about the perils of standing on the edge. Signs tell tales of tourists who died taking photographs, voyeuristic snaps of people teetering on the cliff, an attempt to publicly shame people into behaving. Slabs of slate in worn squares and rectangles cover the sides of the rocky path, passing over small streams where the water flows to the sea. Beneath me the rock formations are stepped gradually down, marked by natural pools in which seagulls bathe. A portal tomb appears to my left, alone in a field.

Baba and Cait in *The Country Girls* are completely embedded in the rural landscape in which they live – based on the fields and lanes of O'Brien's childhood home of Drewsboro, in the village of Tuamgraney, by the shores of Lough Derg, just an hour's drive from here. In her much later 2012 memoir, *The Country Girl*, she writes of how, as a child, nature and her desire to write were intertwined. She would admire the prose of a local journalist who described these same sea cliffs I am walking, but felt the leafy nature of her own countryside home of Drewsboro to be surely unmatched anywhere in the world. *The Country Girls*' opening page speaks of the daisies on the lawn, the dew everywhere and the mist on the outer field of the house. I know how it feels, this love of a house embedded in nature – I often feel it for my parents' house in Sligo, although I didn't grow up there, so I can only imagine the wonder of a country childhood.

One of the passages that most offended people takes place in the elm grove near the house in which Cait grows up, where the two girls secretly explore each other's bodies – Baba using the illicit encounter as leverage in their friendship, so that Cait is forced to produce new silk hankies or ribbons to keep Baba's confidence. Reading it, I was struck by how nature and sexuality seem to be intertwined. O'Brien was daring to suggest not only that women might enjoy sex, might desire it and seek it out, but even that female desire might be sexually fluid. Later, under the regime of an oppressively strict convent, Cait forms a romantic attachment to a young nun, before she and Baba are both expelled and are free to move to Dublin.

The novel was lauded in London and New York, but was immediately banned in Ireland, fuelled, as O'Brien mentions in her own memoir, by the censorship of the then archbishop of Dublin, Charles McQuaid. Ireland at that time was a country still very much under the sway of the Catholic Church, the men who controlled it and the male politicians who colluded in its power. *The Country Girls* shattered an idealised view of virtuous, chaste femininity, of the family package that Ireland sold its women – an ideal, I am beginning to realise, that might have impacted my own life as well. *The Country Girls* told of an Ireland behind closed doors – of drunken, feckless fathers who beat their children and young women seeing both casual suitors and married men. O'Brien received anonymous letters telling her to drown in her own filth. The post-mistress in Tuamgraney said that she should be kicked naked through the street.

Edna O'Brien was born in 1930, and when the Irish constitution was written in 1937, it enshrined that mothers 'shall not be obliged by economic necessity to engage in labour to the neglect of their duties in the home', reinforcing the gender stereotype that men should be the main breadwinners. And in post-war England, too, this was very much the status quo. It is hard for me, probably for any woman of my generation, to imagine how limiting life must have felt. The very writing of *The Country Girls* was an act of defiance. Through its creation Edna O'Brien had escaped from a suburban life in late 1950s London, where she had found herself trapped in an unhappy marriage with an older man, the writer Ernest Gébler.

Gébler, O'Brien again writes in her autobiography, was a controlling person who maintained a running commentary on his wife's movements in a log book he kept locked in his study. While reading her autobiography I found myself distressed, not only by the behaviour she describes, but also to learn that O'Brien's husband had to counter-sign her royalty cheques for her to access the funds. I was astounded to discover that it wasn't until 1975, just a year before the ITV documentary was made, and four years before I was born, that women in the UK and Ireland could open a bank account in their own name. O'Brien describes how part of her own marriage breakdown was because her literary success was a threat to this status quo. She was in many ways a better writer than Gébler and wrote about things her husband did not like. Her three-year custody battle over her children saw him trying to paint her in the London courts as an unfit mother by reading excerpts from her novel *August Is a Wicked Month*. Thankfully, the judge saw through it.

It's nearing noon now and I've spent almost an hour walking – looking down on black rocks and whirlpools. Waves form and break out in the ocean, huge swathes of foam forming round the shoreline. I cross over a wooden and mesh stile, two large boulders placed at either side. There are thistles, purple and bulbous, along the path here and little yellow bird's foot trefoil among the dandelions and clover. The wind is so high it whips round me with a whistle. A ray of sunlight peeps through overhead, and I will with all my might for it to be an indication that the day is softening, that the rain forecast earlier will hold off. The main cliffs I reckon to be still an hour or so's walking distance from here.

Mother Ireland, written sixteen years and seven novels after *The Country Girls*, seems at first glance like a travelogue, but it soon became clear to me that O'Brien is actually walking the landscape of memory, recalling her early life in Clare – the men who flash you from behind hedges, the heroic Irish tales taught in the classroom, the convent, the eventual move to Dublin. Interviewed in the 1976 ITV documentary, she speaks about how it was difficult to write, as she was used to fiction rather than fact. Like my own mother and father in the 1970s, when Edna O'Brien wrote *Mother Ireland* she was living in London, and the distance allowed her to explore the idea of Ireland – the Ireland of her mind. Reading *Mother Ireland* as the daughter of Irish immigrants, her Ireland seems somehow suspended in time, as in the book she admits that, despite having been away for almost twenty years, she still spends a great deal of time ruminating on this place that treated her so very poorly. 'Time changes everything including our attitude to a place,' she writes. 'There is no such thing as a perpetual hatred no more than there are unambiguous states of earthly love.'

My parents, twenty years younger than O'Brien, left Ireland in the late 1960s. Sometimes I wonder if, throughout their thirty-five years in London, they had somehow distilled a 1960s Ireland to which they would one day return? When they did, in 2001, I felt that we all had something of a reawakening. Ireland was in the middle of rapid economic growth and I watched them adapt to the country Ireland had become while they were away. I spent, for the first time in my life, a full summer and autumn in Sligo – the year after I graduated. I felt conflicted – I was irritated that I no longer had a home in London while I struggled to find my feet, but I also remember discovering the beauty of watching the seasons pass. I remember how much I came to love the yellow bog irises that grew at the end of the next field to our house, how I watched in fascination the hay-baling machine at work as it cleared the land.

The Cliffs of Moher – iconic, huge, black and intimidating – reveal themselves in the distance, nosing out to sea. Spots of rain begin to appear. There's a small green telescope on a grassy bank and I put a euro in, continuing my now daily quest to see dolphins or whales. On the way back to Dunquin Harbour, the couple I'd shared Peig's house with had casually mentioned that they'd seen a whale on their own walk around the Great Blasket and it left me with a feeling of being somehow short-changed, so I keep persisting, staring out at the horizon as I walk, for an hour or more, along the edge, the main cliffs drawing ever nearer. Now I deviate from the path with the other tourists as the cliffs become more and more spectacular, seeking the best photograph in the face of the shearing wind until, all at once, the weather breaks. The mist rolls in, takes over and soon it's raining so heavily that within minutes I am soaked. The sea, the cliffs, the rocks beneath are merely a blank space to my right.

I walk through an impenetrable white mist while it pours down upon me, unable to see further than a metre in any direction. It has all happened so fast, I think, as I come to the formless shape of what must be a building, only realising it is O'Brien's Tower once I am upon it. Here, at the highest point of the cliffs, I'd hoped to take in the panorama that Edna O'Brien enjoyed, but this is a now ludicrous aim. I search around the tower for the entrance, only to find a formless mass of people crowded in at the doorway, like some many-limbed animal. I've no option but to continue walking until I can find shelter.

Ten minutes later I'm in the ladies toilets at the glass-walled visitor centre, completely soaked to the skin. I dry my face, hands and legs as well as I can, and in the canteen I hang my rain jacket on the back of a chair before I queue with the other tourists to buy a hearty, overpriced lunch of pure carbohydrate on a red plastic tray. I eat crowded onto another table with a distracted freelancer who seeks to tell me about her nascent marketing business while the rain steams up the windows of the restaurant. This is not the Cliffs of Moher walk I had in mind. It is also the first time on this journey that I have truly felt like a tourist. Of course I *know* that I am a tourist, but I haven't felt like one until now.

In *Mother Ireland* O'Brien describes the 1970s Irish tourist experience, paralleling my own with her unflinching eye – the white cottages, blue hazy mountains and fuchsia lanes of Kerry:

> the chalky limestone steppes of West Clare, a phenomenon so unyielding it is as if Wuthering Heights were transmitted from paper to a landscape. The visitors talk and are talked at, they fish, they fowl, they eat brown bread, dip into holy wells, kiss wishing stones but have no

desire to stay. There must be something secretly
catastrophic about a country from which so
many people go, escape.

She is right, of course, about the leaving – the numbers,
the wakes for those going to America, show it to be true.
And she is right about the tourist experience. My walk
along the cliffs has been an unyielding phenomenon,
that's for sure, but it's more down to the Irish weather
than the cliffs themselves today.

If anything, my problem at the moment seems to be
that I can't stop coming to Ireland, consumed by what
has become an obsession, researching the lives of these
women and walking along this coast. It's a few weeks
into my trip now, and my friends back home are beginning to feel a bit neglected – where am I, they're asking,
as I miss summer barbecues and open-air concerts. It's
a nice feeling to be wanted – especially when part of the
reason for this trip was that I felt like I was a bit out of
step with the young families springing up all around me,
that I might have a long summer of not much ahead of
me. It's a reminder that the stories we tell ourselves are
often of our own making.

As a child on holiday, I used to think that it rained
heavily in Ireland *all the time*. In fact, this is my first day
in a month that it has rained torrentially, and now it has
stopped. Outside the visitor centre, people from across
the globe pose for pictures against the white space of pure
fog where the cliffs should be. This must be a common
occurrence because inside the centre there is a digital
booth where you can be photographed against the sheer
drop. I continue my walk along the cliffs without the

spectacular view I was hoping for, the wind whipping me dry. I am simply a body moving through blank nothingness. I could be walking in any landscape. I could be walking in a dream.

I'm grateful for the protected groove of the path, a few feet from the cliff edge, bordered by huge flagstones, pieces of Moher slate hewn from the deposits that lie along these cliffs. All around me is the sweet smell of clover battered by rainfall, and within a matter of minutes the fog starts to lift, as fast as it arrived. Behind me, I can see for the first time this main section of the cliffs in all their glory – the huge rough faces and the great sea stack of Branaunmore, left behind by the relentless waves that crash against these cliffs incessantly, as they have done for millions of years. Out on the ocean, the sea and sky are the same colour – only a silver sheen shows a thin line between them. People start to get closer to the edge again, and I walk past tourists in dubious positions – one lying down to take photos of the precipitous drop, another sitting on a ledge. Two tourists in front of me hold hands as they pose at the very edge of the cliff, and I feel myself involuntarily gasp. They smile up at me. 'We're fine,' says the man. 'It's not as bad as it looks.' I pass what must be an old quarry – a large bowl cut out of the rock on the clifftop, where rain has collected in a sandy pool, next to which people have taken the slates and stacked them into dolmens.

As I head south, the amount of tourists dwindles until there's just me and one other, a man coming the opposite way. He stops to chat as we pass, wondering aloud, 'How do they get the flagstones so thin?' As I continue walking, I find the answer – a large wall of exposed rock where I can see the formations up close and the squiggly lines of fossilised sea creatures within them. The geological layers of a 300-million-year-old basin, normally only visible under the sea, exposed as a result of a plate collision. Sheets of thin sedimentary rock built up over time, now splintering to reveal each separate layer of sandstone, siltstone or shale – some red, some black, some orange or brown, and over all of it a sandy wash upon which fossilised animals and wave ripples are left behind. Hag's Head is now in sight, but as I walk towards it, the mist rolls back in and the cliffs start to vanish again. I sit down to rest and, seeing me scribbling in my notebook, some Americans passing by ask if I am casting a spell, if I am the witch that controls the weather. I reply that I am. They stop and rest beside me and their Irish guide, perhaps also for my benefit, describes how there are hags all over Ireland – women who were turned to stone. I dislike the word *hag*, I realise as he speaks. It sounds old and ugly, suggestive of someone slightly crazed, chaotic and prone to meddling.

By the time I reach Hag's Head my feet are aching. On the headland, Japanese tourists pose in front of the ruined Napoleonic signal tower, taking photos of the craggy rock. I walk on a little further to where a group of people are gathered as if at a ceremony. At first I wonder if they are saying mass but then I hear cheers. The door of a vintage car decorated with ribbons opens and a woman in white steps out. I surprise myself, expecting to feel cynical but actually seeing it as a sign of hope – thinking of this bride and groom having waited for the rain to pass before they can have their ceremony. I turn my back on them, walk towards the signal tower behind the Hag where I rest my feet again. The sun is shining now and my clothes are almost dry. I feel like I've been through a wash and spin cycle before being tumble-dried by the elements. The three Aran Islands, where I am headed next, are now so clear that I can spot the white houses on them.

The Hag of Beara that I passed back in Kerry, that Edna O'Brien put forward as one of the aspects of Mother Ireland, is, in fact, a natural volcanic boulder cast adrift in an otherwise granite landscape, said to be the remains of the woman herself. Her story is told in the poem 'The Lament of the Hag of Beare' from the twelfth century. In verse, she tells of how she has been ravaged over time, how once she wore bright clothes, took lovers and drank mead and wine with kings, was round bodied and fair skinned but is now a veiled, shriv-elled old hag at prayer, as described in this translation by Eleanor Hull:

> Ebb tide to me!
> My life drifts downward with the drifting sea;
> Old age has caught and compassed me about,
> The tides of time run out.

I find myself connecting Peig Sayers's old-woman persona and the old hag's lament, and I feel all at once grateful to live in a time and place where the expectations of age are moving and shifting. Reading Edna O'Brien's work and looking at how her life was documented and her work received, I have been overwhelmingly reminded of something important. Something so obvious that it's easy to forget. That the personal is political – what a woman does with her body, with her mind, with her money is only recently, in Ireland as well as in the UK, her own choice. One of the most galling moments in the *Mother Ireland* documentary comes at the end, as the interviewer asks Edna O'Brien, 'What do you most regret about your life?' when she's only forty-five years old! This idea that, for women, once you have reached a certain age the best is over angers me, knowing that there's another forty years of writing ahead for Edna O'Brien after this moment captured on film – that she is still writing now. Edna O'Brien changed, is changing, perceptions for the women who will follow. Her reply to the question is just perfect. 'My life?' she says. 'I wish it had been funnier.'

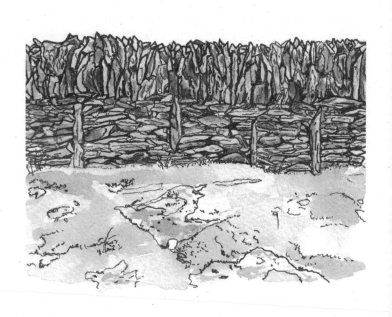

7. ON ARAN

Úna McDonagh
Inisheer, County Galway

It's the end of July now and I am sea-lashed on the hooker out to Inishmore, or, in Irish, Inis Mór. I'm with my cousin Orla, whom I picked up in Galway to travel out to the Aran Islands with me, and we have been hit by a relentless downpour. White sheets of water so huge that we are soaked to the skin in minutes; the sea rising and falling in great mountains. Orla looks more unwell than I have ever seen her, more unwell even than in 2016 when we both experienced, for the first time, the choppy waters around Cape Clear. We are lucky the hooker is even running, the skipper tells me, as I grip the iron handrails on deck as if my life depends on it, my stomach travelling between my throat and my feet. There's a stag party from Dublin on the boat with us, and I concentrate on breathing in and out as one of them chats away to me, flirting and commenting on the fine shape of my legs to entertain the rest, while Orla stares out at the horizon, pale and silent.

An hour later, drenched and in shock, we sit over a bowl of hot chowder in one of the island's three pubs, where a Mayo vs. Meath All-Ireland Gaelic football match plays on the TV in the corner. Sitting there, sodden, our feet like ice and our bones cold, Orla confides in me that we have just undergone one of the most extreme weather experiences of her life and, I have to agree, of mine too. Two days ago, at the Galway Arts Festival, we had listened rapt as the former president of Ireland Mary Robinson gave a talk about climate change, to promote her book *Climate Justice*, about how the weather in Ireland is evolving as sea levels rise. Storms along the west coast have always occurred, but they are becoming more frequent. Now, it is as if Orla and I are seeing this first-hand. It continues to rain for hours. All day and all night. Extraordinary, torrential rain that we watch transfixed through the large glass window of the Aran Walkers Lodge while our walking shoes sit stuffed full of newspaper, drying on the radiator. My notebook begins to fill up with scribbled ferry times and bed and breakfasts as we extend our stay by another night and I let Úna McDonagh – a traditional knitter whom I have arranged to meet on Inisheer, or Inis Oírr, the Arans' smallest island – know that I'll be a day late.

After weeks alone, walking around Inishmore with Orla the next day, the weather now at drizzle level, feels like a gift – the joy of time together just walking and talking, away from any kind of distraction. We have a lot in common as well as our family connection – a passion for art and a child-free, independent life. We usually only see each other in the city and it's good to reconnect here, in Ireland, in nature – something we haven't

done since that weekend on Cape Clear. Although Orla
was brought up in Foynes (it was she who had told me
about the work of Charlotte Grace O'Brien), for a long
time we palled about in London, where she moved in her
twenties to further her career in healthcare. A few years
ago she had a Damascene moment and decided to move
back to the west coast to retrain as an artist, and now
she divides her time between Galway and London.

We follow the path from the Walkers Lodge down
to the deserted sandy crescent of Cill Muirbhthe –
Kilmurvey – on the northern shores of the island, where
I head into the sea while Orla beachcombs. I swim vig-
orously, getting out after twenty minutes, shivering, and
as I change, Orla shows me some rocks that she's found
on her walk. One seems so alive, she tells me, that she's
almost frightened of it. When I see it, I understand why
– a clump of sediment compacted together into stones,
weathered old shells and what seems to be the bright
pink and yellow remains of an octopus tentacle.

Our aim for the afternoon is to walk to Pol na bPéist,
or the Wormhole – Inishmore's famous natural rock pool
that lies under the cliff of the fort at Dun Aengus. It's a
place I learnt about as I had Maude Delap: through an
artwork by the contemporary artist Dorothy Cross.
The artwork is a photograph of a woman floating, naked,
in a huge, perfectly rectangular pool in the limestone
rock. The Wormhole is a geological wonder, formed by
nature into a remote, tempting swimming spot that ebbs
and flows with the tides that fill and empty the pool
from underneath. It seems the ultimate expression of
freedom, of giving in to the sea. I want to see it with my
own eyes. I want to swim in it.

We take the long way round – a looped walk across Inishmore's eastern half. It is still raining, but only gently. Blue harebells grow on the sides of the road; two brown donkeys bat their lashes over a metal gate so invitingly that we have to pet them. There are coffee cups and plastic bottles on the sides of the paths from the thousands of tourists like ourselves that come to the Aran Islands, and especially Inishmore, every year. Day trippers pass us along the road, wobbling on their hired bikes. We're the only people walking and it is meditative, putting one foot in front of the other in a steady rhythm.

After initial puzzlement over my enthusiasm for Peig Sayers, Orla is now excited by the idea that I am discovering Ireland, is incredibly supportive of my trip, and I feed from her enthusiasm as she points out the names of the plants for me in Irish, only one of which I remember now – an buachalán buí, yellow ragwort, covered in little yellow and black cinnabar caterpillars. Across the water, we can see Connemara beyond the brown seaweed that has formed a low-tide barrier against the sea. The sun comes out and we take off our jackets as Orla tells me about her life in Galway City where she's hired an art studio, developing her work in order to put together the portfolio she'll need to apply to the Royal College of Art. It would mean a move back to London again and she would miss Galway now, she says, while I tell her about my adventures of the past few weeks.

Deep into the southern part of Inishmore, we follow a small track covered in cow parsley until we reach a sign – a piece of slate on which the words 'Poll na bPéist' are handwritten in white paint. The entrance to the Wormhole path, if you can call it that, is marked by two long rectangular limestone stones placed upright to form a gap in the wall, before which, on the ground, another large rock – possibly granite rather than limestone – has been placed as a gate-stone. Next to it, against the wall, two bicycles have been abandoned by their renters who must be ahead of us. We contemplate moving them to the other side of the wall, just for the sake of mischief, but in the end decide we are far too mature for that sort of thing and, squeezing through the gap, we follow the makeshift track that has somehow formed in a field that is half grass and half stone. This is the low road to the Wormhole, a couple we meet coming the other way tells us, but there's a high road too, from the fort on top of the cliffs. The acres of fields are now an expanse of pure karst limestone. Occasionally we come across an erratic – a lichen-clad granite rock or boulder dumped here onto the landscape ten thousand years ago when, at the end of the last Ice Age, the ice melted.

I'm realising as we walk how much I've missed company and laughter. At a section where the stone is incredibly flat I find myself looking at the names that people have scratched into the stone – DYLAN KITT, SEAN AND SARAH, MO + LO, ROSSA MCCABE and in huge letters simply JONNY. Some people alone, some together – all feeling a need to leave a mark, however impermanent. The sea is cyan, the waves rolling in towards the shore. As if to mock our sliding, faltering progress, an elderly man appears with a stick. A daily walk, he tells us – he has to get out, after all. The cliffs rise above us. Here at their base, a long hollow cave has formed, eroded by millennia of waves hitting the side of the shore and creating a ledge that juts forward and upon which it's possible to see the layers of sandstone. We've timed this badly and now the waves are coming in, washing against the rock face a few metres away. We gingerly cross the hard, uneven and slippery surface, carefully placing one foot in front of the other. We are filled with excited anticipation, and just at the point where we can no longer stand upright under the cliffs, our reward for slow progress appears – the Wormhole.

It is a true marvel – fifteen metres long and five or six metres wide, a perfect rectangular swimming pool cut into the rock bed. We stare down into the bottom, where the ocean surges in and out, the dark turquoise water propelled forward by the tide, exploding into white. The idea that I could swim here is ridiculous and, many people have told us since we arrived on the island, much ill-advised. The water washes up and down with the force of an entire ocean inside the straight walls of the pool. The air is filled with spray and the noise is immense; we have to shout to be heard above it as we stand mesmerised, watching the surface as it rises and falls with the power of the waves that swell from underneath. The wind is high, the sea becoming rougher, and we're scared to stand too close as we pose for photographs. I will come to treasure these pictures later as evidence that we were here, knowing that they will increase in meaning as the years pass, and I feel sad to say goodbye to Orla the next day on Kilronan Pier, waving her off on board the ferry back to Rossaveal.

It has been over too soon – I leave Orla clutching a rusted cow-shed lamp that she found on the side of the road on our way back to the Walkers Lodge, which she thinks she might one day use in an artwork. After a complex negotiation with tickets, I get back on board the hooker, where the stag party I met on the way over are on the same boat, heading back to the mainland after my stop at Inisheer. They seem pale and broken now by their weekend of excess, and the man who flirted with me a few days ago is suddenly shy now that I'm alone.

*

On arriving at Inisheer, I find Úna McDonagh immediately behind the till at the café that she and her family run next to the harbour. A traditional knitter, Úna was born and raised here on the smallest of the Aran Islands, where she still lives. While Ellen Cotter may have made lace, my own mother is a skilled knitter and in turn taught me, starting me out on a lifelong journey. The way we knit reflects our personalities. My mother is prolific – she loves to continuously knit the same pattern, whether hats or cardigans, churning out shop-loads of beautifully crafted items. I knit maybe one or two things a year, but push myself to do something different each time, meaning I constantly have to unravel and reknit. I've only just got the hang of socks, and I'm thinking of moving past basic plain and purl to the intricate, complicated stitch patterns that Aran jumpers, or in Irish *geansaí Árann*, are made up of.

Coming here, to the Aran Islands, is an opportunity for me to understand more about what is surely the most famous women's work in Ireland and maybe pick up a few new stitches. The Arans have traditionally been perceived by outsiders, from the Irish writer J. M. Synge to the British sculptor Richard Long, as a place where an older way of life – of the kind Peig Sayers would have seen – has been preserved away from mainland Ireland, and I'm curious to reflect on how women lived in this landscape. To understand, in more of a physical way – through clothes and wool and work – what life would have been like.

When I reached out to Úna, I couldn't work out at first, as our emails went back and forth across the weeks, why it seemed hard to pin down an actual meeting date, but now – having just spent the past three days at the mercy of the unpredictable weather system around these islands – I know that time is different here. It has a sliding, sea-dependent quality that I didn't quite understand.

Once I've been sufficiently restored with coffee and homemade cake, Úna takes me up to the island's arts centre to look at an exhibition of clothing curated by some of the island women. It shows the traditional clothes that the people on Inisheer once wore – the wool trousers on one of the mannequins are those of Úna's own grandfather Mairtín Shearraigh. The clothing of the Aran islanders evolved over centuries to reflect both the available raw materials and the physically demanding nature of their work in this unpredictable climate, and they marked the islanders out when they visited the mainland. Homespun woollen clothes were common once in Ireland, Úna tells me. The distinctive blue and red skirts were worn by women throughout the west coast at one time or another, not simply on the Aran Islands. But traditional dress – including the Galway shawl – persisted longer on these islands than in any other part of Ireland, right up into the 1980s.

The same clothes seen and recorded by Synge and the other writers and ethnographers who flocked here in the late-nineteenth century.

Úna shows me an example of the soft shoes – *bróga úrleathair*, or papooties, as they were known – made of raw cowhide or, in earlier times, seal skin and kept damp to stay soft. A protection against the roughness of the ground, they were worn hairy-side out for grip on the rocks along the west coast of Ireland. 'They only lasted about a month and they had to be soaked at night,' Úna tells me. She remembers, as a child in the 1970s, a few older men still wearing them on the beach, launching currachs in the same way they had done in the 1930s. But when rubber boots arrived things changed, and by 1980, she says, everyone on the island was wearing shoes.

My favourite, I decide, of all the traditional clothing the women made is the beautiful *crios*, a brightly coloured belt, the plural of which is *criosanna*. These were made of wool, in bright reds, oranges, yellows and greens with black and white trim. The men's version was three and a half yards in length – over three metres – and, wrapped around, provided back support as they worked. They look to me almost South American, but in fact are a feature of traditional Irish costume – woven by hand with the thread stretched between two chairs or stools or, more traditionally, between one hand and one foot so that they could be made anywhere.

An hour or so later, in Úna's sitting room, she explains that there's always been knitting on these islands. Before needles arrived, Girls learnt to knit with the spines of goose feathers, because they were strong and flexible. The island sheep were sheared before their fleeces were sent to Galway, where they were washed and carded. The Aran wool would then be sold, with some of it coming back to the island's households to be spun into wool to weave or knit with. Every woman on the island could knit – making socks for the army had been pin money for generations of women. Úna produces the small needles she'll use to teach me some of the more complex stitch patterns that I want to learn, and a ball of yellow wool that smells of lanolin – the natural waxy coat of the sheep – and leaves a slight residue on my hands.

'A true Aran jumper has a slight yellow colour. They kept the oils in for water repellence. The more you wash it, the less oily it gets, but out on fishing boats all day you need those oils to keep you dry.'

Úna also shows me a photograph from 1934 of some little boys wearing Aran jumpers that they would have been given on their First Holy Communion, around the age of six or seven. Those first jumpers would have been made from the first fleece of a lamb – the whitest wool, called in Irish *báinín*, 'little white' – to be worn to mass on Sundays. Although the origin of the Aran jumper as we know it is slightly lost to time, it probably dates from the late 1890s and the national drive by the British government's Congested Districts Board, post-Famine, to find employment for people along the western seaboard – the same scheme that brought my own great-grandmother to teach lacemaking on Cape Clear.

It wasn't until the 1950s that the Aran knitting industry as we know it really took off, when Pádraig Ó Síocháin, a Cork-born journalist, began selling Aran jumpers in Galway town and later exporting them to the American and Canadian markets. Úna told me the story goes that when Ó Síocháin first brought the wool to the women of the island, he just gave it out to anyone who was interested and asked them to knit. They came back with perfect sweaters, but each was unique according to its knitter and wearer. If a woman's husband or children were petite, she was used to knitting smaller, shorter clothing. If she had a tall family, she added in a few extra rows. This is one of the pleasures of knitting I have always found – that I can adapt to a short shoulder or a long arm as necessary. But of course, that doesn't work in the shops, so soon the islanders evolved a standard sizing and the business took off, the patterns becoming more and more elaborate with different twists and cables and the women being paid by the ounce. 'The women took it over and made it their own then,' Úna tells me. 'It's like every art, I think – you are going to be always experimenting and chopping and changing.'

Back then, life on the island was labour intensive. Each family raised their own cattle or fished, and they grew their own vegetables. Tourism wasn't the big business it is now, and apart from a few roadworks schemes there wasn't a lot of work. When the opportunity came to be able to knit to order, Úna tells me, it had a huge impact on the economy. A good week's work would knit an Aran jumper. 'You wouldn't do much else but people were very fast knitting back then because they were used to knitting for their families.' Soon Ó Síocháin had problems keeping up with demand, as the Aran jumper became Hollywood A-list chic. Grace Kelly wore one in 1950, and by 1956 an Aran pattern was published by *Vogue*. Steve McQueen wore one, as did JFK. Marilyn

Monroe even danced in one in the film *Let's Make Love*, made in 1960. The popularity meant that a handknitting industry on the Arans would continue into the 1980s, and of course, still today there are handknits for sale on the islands.

It was a turnaround for a garment that was primarily to clothe families – they were passed on and upscaled from child to child. 'You could pull a thread here and add a piece or add a different colour for the next one,' says Úna, as she shows me how a traditional Aran sweater is put together. The pattern is split into thirds – the front and back have one main centre panel, and then the sides are patterned as a mirror image of each other, with the stitches that feature on the sleeves repeated in the centre. Úna's started me on a blackberry or trinity stitch and now we're onto the chain stitch, which involves twisting the stitches in front of each other so they form borders around the plain knit. I use a cable needle to hold my stitches in place before I move them across to form the cable, but Úna is so experienced she just leaves hers hanging in the air and picks them up when she needs them, her skill both natural and effortless. I ask her if she remembers learning to knit. 'I was five, I think,' she tells me. 'I wasn't able to cast on – but I was able to knit plain-stitch clothes for my dolls. I was the only one that could already knit out of my class. I remember that distinctly.'

To cast on, for the uninitiated, means to create the first row of knitting. It was not until she was seven or eight that Úna learnt to do that. Knitting was on the curriculum, and the girls learnt to knit while the boys sat in the other room of the school, playing board games or reading or doing their homework. I think it's a shame, I tell Úna – some of the boys might have enjoyed knitting? 'True enough. We were jealous of them anyway, not having to learn.' In fourth class, at about the age of ten, the girls would have to make their first Aran jumper.

They would start in September with the intention of someone in the family wearing it to midnight mass on Christmas Eve, so that everyone's work was displayed. A huge task for those who were not natural knitters, I say to Úna. My own mother has often told me the story of how her grandmother turned the heel on her socks so that she never learnt how to do it herself, but Úna says the teacher would have known if you got help. 'I mean, it was something I was good at so I wouldn't even think of getting Mum to do it for me. But I'm sure if people were struggling that did happen.' Úna made her three-year-old sister Rita a red Aran, with honeycomb at the front and cables and a little bit of moss stitch. 'I can still see it. I was delighted because it was small and I had it well finished by Christmas, and the following year I did one for myself.' There was, of course, huge praise.

As I struggle with my stitches, Úna picks up a book from the pile she has put aside for me – a *National Geographic* magazine from April 1971 with a cover story, third billing, called 'Ireland's Invincible Isles' by Veronica Thomas. Thomas stands apart as a pioneer – a lone female writer on the five listed features of the month, which range from a piece on orchids to 'Hungary: Changing Homeland of a Tough Romantic People', through to 'Polar Bear: Lonely Nomad of the North'. I put down my knitting to flick through the magazine. At first glance it appears to be of its time – a snapshot of how white, moneyed America once saw the rest of the world. Úna points to a photograph in the middle of the Aran story, and there, in the corner, is a little girl sitting on her mother's knee. It's five-year-old Úna, dressed in red. She partly hides her face in the lap of her smiling mother, timidly eyeing the camera, while her eleven-year-old brother grins into it. The caption names Úna's father, Colman Conneely, and his wife, Moira, along with their two children.

A newspaper is open in front of Úna's Aunt Mary, with a pair of glasses set to one side. The room reminds me of my Sligo grandparents' home in the 1980s – the black range, wallpaper darkened from the burning of coal and the sacred heart of Jesus hanging up above them all. Úna's father looks relaxed, her mother proud. Úna remembers it clearly. Her brother Padraic had told her that when they took the photograph a claw would come out of the camera. 'I look scared because I was waiting for the claw. That's why I'm hiding – I was terrified.' Veronica Thomas and the *National Geographic* photographer Winfield Parks had stayed with them on their visit. I leaf through the article, full of joy at the photographs.

'Her description of the islands is very true to the time,' Úna says. 'It really is. Even P. J. Mullan coming over in the boat, like – he used to brave the seas in the worst conditions, and all that is very true. She describes him well, you know, she really does.' Úna points out the photograph of the sailor who brought Veronica Thomas over, with a bright blue eyes and a cigarette hanging out of his mouth.

We lean over the magazine together, with Úna telling me who she remembers from the photographs. The Dutch weaver of *criosanna* whom the islanders called 'The Dane'. He lived at the house at the end of the beach

– Úna's father used to deliver gas to him, she tells me. There's a beautiful photograph of a school – the children scrubbed up and smiling at the camera. 'That's on Inishmaan. But I can relate to that. I remember the timber biros, those yellow timber biros. And the jackets, those checked jackets on the boys.'

I recognise a photograph of a pub that must be famous – four half-drunk pints of Guinness on a table in front of a window, on the other side of which three men in flat caps stand. 'There's a funny bit where Veronica's sitting in the pub,' says Úna. 'She starts giggling because she was nervous – because women wouldn't be in the pub. But then once the ice was broken, sure, she was part of it all. She bought them a few drinks.'

Back in London, months later, I find myself looking up Veronica Thomas, who died aged eighty-two in 2011. Born in Limerick, in May 1950, she had travelled to New York on the *Queen Mary* with ambitions to become a journalist and had succeeded. She wrote for a seventies American food magazine called *Gourmet* as well *National Geographic*. Her obituary in *The Irish Times* mentioned that she had rather fabulously dated Marlon Brando, but met her husband while covering the opening of the Hilton Jamaica. I find myself envying her life – she lived next door to Miles Davis on Manhattan's Upper West Side and once told him off for playing his trumpet, as her son was trying to sleep.

I track down a copy of the magazine and read her article in full. Thomas begins in a hotel in Galway, where she worries that the Aran people might not speak to her because she is a woman. Advised by a priest that buying a few pints of porter makes most people friendly, she makes her way across the three Aran Islands via a steamer, the *Naomh Eanna*, where she develops a crush on the captain, Leo Tynan. Thomas undertakes an almost exact replica of my own trip, from visiting Dun Aengus on Inishmore, a choppy boat ride and being caught in endless rain, to meeting a traditional knitter, Margaret Flaherty. On the boat with P. J. Mullan, they encounter a wave so big that she can't see the top of it, watches a man called Peter Gillen fish off the cliffs, is laughed at by the lighthouse keepers for visiting, who then give her some lobster, fresh from the pot. Here on Inisheer, the sun comes out for her at last, and she walks by the rocky shore while a white pony trots along the main road of the island.

Reading it on my own in London, I find Thomas's article to be unashamedly romantic, mentioning the 'aristocratic nature' of the people she meets, and as I read, I wonder if it must be quite wearing as an Aran islander to be constantly seen and written about as the inhabitants of an idealised far-flung place by people passing through. In a recent Irish travel book that inspired my own journey, Rebecca Solnit's *Migrations*, written when she got her Irish passport, she decides not to visit the Arans because of these stereotypes. But when I ask Úna, on a much later visit, if she thinks that Thomas falls into romanticism, she's not convinced. 'Oh, reading it, it brings back a lot of memories. It is very accurate for sure. Don't think she romanticises it unless I'm looking back with rose-coloured glasses. No, I think it's very true to how things were.'

On that first visit, I get as far as I can with my tangled knitting and leave Úna with a promise to return. Perhaps, she says, if I come again, she'll take some measurements and we can knit me a cardigan. She encourages me to bring my mother's old one from the 1980s to see if we can adapt it to fit me. 'We can do some – what do they call it? – upcycling. Because that's very important now. They are family heirlooms, so we could do some adjustments.'

My walk the next day takes me around the entire ring of the island, in a circle from the pier that Úna had showed me a photograph of her Aunty Nonie knitting next to. She used to sit there on the rocks, she told me, her two needles clicking as she sat watching the comings and goings of the island. Now the tourist ferries dock here, and I walk past a line of people buying fudge and coffees from one of the stalls, while outside a pub on the harbour, lobster pots are stacked – each cage weighed down with a single large flat stone.

Around the north-western corner of the island, the sloping form of Inishmaan – the middle of the three Aran Islands – appears out on the Atlantic horizon. Over the flat flags of limestone, I cross back onto the main path. The different levels of stone walls, in almost fort-like rings, rise into the centre of the island. Walking alone, the sparse beauty of this landscape, of cracked stones and patchy fields, comes into its own. It's hard and unrelenting, yet Úna's work in wool, so intricate and ultimately fragile, exists within it, as a response to it. At either side of me are the drystone walls that have been a revelation to me since I arrived on the Aran Islands five days ago. The islands are criss-crossed by walls, Úna told me, because the stones they are made of were once cast across the fields. The early islanders built the walls to clear the land and make it fit for grazing or crops, which is why the Aran fields are often smaller than average. I marvel at the artistry of the wall constructions: the careful selection of stones and how they fit together; the intricate, repetitious patterns created by the different shapes and colours of the limestone. By how precariously balanced the smallest rocks often appear, yet are sturdier than you could imagine.

I had told my cousin Orla while we walked that I would never get tired of looking at them. She agreed with me about the harmony, the beauty of the lines. 'But, you know, when I look at them I also see hunger,' she said, as I stopped to take yet another photograph on my phone. They reminded her, she explained, of pointless work set by landlords in return for very little – famine walls, like the ones in the Burren, County Clare, that run from the very bottom to the top of mountains, which I did not know about before I started this journey. That served no purpose other than to provide work for starving men employed on schemes run by the Church or landlords. Orla isn't the only Irish person who has mentioned to me how emotional they find these drystone walls, and I begin to wonder if, like Peig's stories, it is only my distance that makes me love them so much?

Úna had told me while we were knitting that what I call the honeycomb cable she calls *bulan* – the Aran Irish word for rock pool. When teaching me how to make cables, where two lines of stitches cross each other, Úna had compared the crossover to the wall around the land. She talked about opening the gap in the stitches, as you would in a stone-wall field – moving the keystone that the cattle would go in and out through, and then closing it again. A kind of storytelling. The pleasure of knitting, it occurs to me, perhaps like the pleasure of building these walls, is in the intricacy, in learning how the stitches stack and then accepting, unravelling, fixing mistakes. As I walk, in my mind anyway, the knitting and the landscape are becoming one.

I don't know quite what I'd expected coming to the Aran Islands. Unlike the Blasket Islands, which I had never heard of until I read Peig Sayers's work and so had no preconceptions, I did have some vague romantic ideal in my head about Aran identity. A simple, self-sufficient, outdoors life of clean living, of masculine hardiness, as depicted in films such as Robert J. Flaherty's 1934 *Man of Aran*, that I also suspected was in some way fake – a myth made up by Hollywood – a kind of rustic authenticity that people in cities yearn for. A vision of old Ireland used to sell jumpers to American tourists. But as I walk here, with Inishmaan a constant presence to my right, it seems to me, in part, that the myth was once true. It was an outdoors life here that did require great resilience from both women and men, and it's humbling to think how for generations people have survived in this landscape defined by limestone. Walking here, I can see the pull of the Arans – why artists, photographers, ethnologists and writers flocked here in the Celtic revival of the early twentieth century, as Ireland asserted its identity alongside the fight for independence.

On my left I pass a row of fishing boats and an over-turned currach, propped up by an oil barrel in its centre. I wave at a tractor coming towards me, exchange greetings with a grandmother pushing a buggy. 'Gorgeous afternoon,' she says. 'Heaven.' The sun comes in and out as I walk, and it would be heaven if it were not for the wind. Although it's died down a little, it's still relentless even on this summer's day. It has such force in it, such personality. Perhaps after a while, a few days, weeks, months, I wouldn't notice? As I continue, the sea's horizon eventually disappears to be replaced by a bank of stones. To my left, the endless grey and green lines of walls and fields begin again.

My walking leads to questions as I pound the stones – am I guilty of romanticising the Arans and this entire western coastline? Isn't it only natural that city dwellers project their own fantasies of a simpler life onto places they don't really know? What would it be like to be part of the 288 people who live here in this island community? Or on Cape Clear? Isn't this why people travel, ultimately – to take a break from the monotony of their own lives by imagining for themselves some bucolic fantasy?

There's no need of a road now. The limestone plateau has formed itself into large expansive slabs. I pass a family – a man and his children, a girl and boy – building a dolmen, a popular tourist occupation if the path around me is anything to go by. Behind me a pony and trap carrying visitors veers off to the left at a junction that I was perhaps supposed to follow, but I've missed the turning and I am glad. I follow the coast road along what is now a rough track, past a lump of rusted metal that was once a trolley or a trailer or some other piece of farm equipment. I stop to wonder at yet another incredible wall, made up of thin slivers of rock placed vertically between large square slabs, acting as supports.

Alone now, for an hour or so, I follow an uphill slope to Ceann na Faochnaí, the headland of the south-western corner of the island. Here, at last, I am sheltered and there is no wind, only the murmur of the sea as it rises and falls from behind the shore walls. I stop for a drink of water and pull up my sleeves to get the sun on my arms. The stone has taken over entirely and there are no fields left, just an endless sea of limestone pockmarked by fossils and shot through with lines of white quartz. Mostly the cracks in the limestone are perfectly straight and rigid, but sometimes, for whatever geological reason, they are frilled and meandering, like the legs of the compass jellyfish I saw washed up on the beach near Bantry. To the right, after so much grey stone, the jade shore appears again.

Around the headland, I turn east, a path marked by an overturned orange wellington boot – a helpful marker placed by a farmer or walker to help strangers like myself. I'm now moving above low cliffs that seem on their lower flanks to be made of sandstone. The limestone is in slabs so huge that they remind me of train platforms, occasionally marked with thin fissures from which slivers of vegetation peep – little cottontail groundsel and brown feather-like reeds grow up out of the cracks in the stone, alongside the daisies and samphire. The track towards the lighthouse at Fardurris Point is indicated by another orange boot – the companion to the one I saw a few minutes back. I stop for a rest, take off my jumper now that the wind has let up. In front of me the Cliffs of Moher have come into view, and to my right, across the water, I face Hag's Head. The Cliffs of Moher are mauve now, here in the evening light.

Gravel has been laid among the stones to show the path to the lighthouse. It's hard walking. On this type of ground you have to watch every step and I'm beginning to tire. I reach the lighthouse compound, circumnavigating the mortared stone walls against which, at the nearest point to the sea, loose rocks have been stacked, so that it's possible, if I wanted, to enter the derelict buildings. But the drop on the other side is a big one and I don't want to risk it, especially alone. Instead, I edge around the striped lighthouse, where the rocks give way to a field. But as I turn the corner, I realise why people have decided to take the risk and jump inside the lighthouse walls. I have missed the stile I needed to cross. It was on the other side of the lighthouse, and now there's no clear way from the field back onto the main walking path, as another high mortared wall lies in the way.

Walkers before me have come up with inventive ways to pass this wall – a metal box as a makeshift stile, a piece of birch propped up diagonally – both of which look like ankle breakers to me. Fine for a tall person, maybe, with long legs that'll ease their drop, but not a five-foot-four woman like myself. Instead, I decide to continue walking through the stony field between the wall and the shore. Passing along this east coast of the island, I see the *Plassey* shipwreck at Gob na Cora lying ahead. Lifted by the force of a storm onto the rocks in 1960, it now sits rusting with dignity. After a good fifteen minutes, I come to a pier, and a red gate leads me back walking through the fields to the island's main road. It's a relief for my feet to be back on a level path, where a few houses in the distance mark the start of habitation again, and I quicken my pace, back past Loch Mór to my bed and breakfast, around on the Lighthouse

Road that cuts back into the island. A new build, owned by a young couple, Úna has told me, newlyweds. I'm grateful for the clean white bed.

My next stop is Roundstone, where I plan to spend the first week of August exploring the travels of British artist Ithell Colquhoun. A painter who dabbled in the occult, she spent a summer in Connemara in 1955. I was told about her work by a photographer friend who thought I might be curious about this almost forgotten woman, who painted richly coloured, mysterious canvases. I bought her travelogue, *The Crying of the Wind*, thinking I would read it on the road. Now in bed, under the duvet, I flick through the book.

My dawning awareness that I'm part of a long line of Brits travelling and writing about Ireland is growing. Online, I stumbled across an article by Tate archivist Darragh O'Donoghue about British artists who had travelled to the west coast of Ireland over the years, including those who were, like me, 'quite Irish', such as sculptor Kenneth Armitage. His mother was from County Longford and, although born in Yorkshire, he kept up a connection with his Irish side throughout his life – in 1939 he had written what O'Donoghue describes as a bit of a 'fan boy' letter to naturalist Robert Lloyd Praeger, arranging to source marble in Connemara. He would eventually make it to Connemara in 1941, visiting his Aunty Elsie, who apparently provided him with huge meals the likes of which were not seen in wartime Britain. Often Brits of non-Irish heritage also came to Ireland in search of what O'Donoghue describes as 'a simplicity and spirituality increasingly lost in a mechanised, modern world', as evidenced in Keith Vaughan's 1954 drawings of currachs in Kerry and Welsh baronet Cedric Morris's staying in what he called a peasant cottage in Connemara in 1936, where he was less than complimentary about what he called the charming but lazy local people.

I'd like to think I have more in common with the 'quite Irish' Armitage than I do with Cedric Morris, but the perception of a British artist travelling the west coast is something I thought I should explore as part of my journey. Now I am not so sure. The idea of Brits abroad in Ireland somehow feels sticky and complex, but it might be worth thinking about. I flick through Colquhoun's account of her travels, past her time in Dublin, her sojourn in Salt Hill, until she reaches Roundstone. My first stop is to swim in a place called Erraloch – the beach where Colquhoun seemed to bathe most of the time. I go to sleep that night praying for good weather, hoping that a few days exploring Connemara and visiting the beaches around Roundstone might restore me.

8. GLASSALA

Kate O'Brien
Roundstone, Connemara, County Galway

The water is translucent. So clear that when I dip my face I can see the forests of kelp beneath – large brown rods with flowers on the top. I'm at Coral Strand in Mannin Bay, Ballyconneely, swimming in the early morning. Here the sand isn't sand at all but calcified red seaweed. When you find big pieces, it does look a bit like coral – pink and knobbly and strangely shaped. For a few minutes, I am the only person in the water – the queen of the bay, with its beauty all to myself. When I parked up the only other vehicle was a yellow van, inside which I could hear people moving around. Soon I'm joined by a younger woman – one of the van dwellers from County Wicklow. Having failed to bring her swimming costume on her weekend away, she swims unashamedly naked, although she was so fast getting in that I wouldn't have known if she hadn't mentioned it. I tell her about the kelp groves under the surface, give her a turn using my swimming goggles so that she can see them. As time passes, more and more people arrive, and she has to choose the right time to get out so as not to offend a group of pensioners who've now appeared. In fact, they take no notice of her but mock my wetsuit so openly that I'm pleased to overhear them complain about being cold while I change in the car.

Despite my best efforts, it's been two summers since I was first here in Connemara, when I did, as I had planned, seek out the places visited by Ithell Colquhoun. I had bathed in the cove at Erraloch, which I found exactly as she described, now the haunt not of British surrealists but four teenage girls in neon and black bikinis who I watched bravely jump off the pier. I swam out through the choppy water to see, in bright sunlight, the views of Inishlacken and Errisbeg that Colquhoun described. I visited the tombolo of Gurteen and Dog's Bay, where my experience was dampened by unyielding rain; I found myself soaked on the strand, watching a hardy windsurfer skim the water before ruinously tumbling into the sea.

I had struggled on, hunting for Letterdyfe House where Colquhoun had stayed, and spent a day walking the island of Inishnee, which lies in the bay beside the village of Roundstone, looking, as Colquhoun had, for an ancient well. She was a liberated and likeable travel companion at first – whipping off her clothes to swim at any opportunity, sunbathing naked in the Letterdyfe woods. There were beautiful passages about walking in her work, and descriptions of landscape and colour that showed her artist's eye. In a particularly memorable passage on Inishnee, she had stopped to draw only for the ink on her page to become splattered by

rain, and on that island I had experienced the sound
of the same wind she had, on an overcast and cloudy
day, the sun intermittently struggling through. What
she had seen as the crying of the wind, I saw more as
a conversation between the elements – the sky, the sea,
the land and the trees.

But as I read and walked and read again, Colquhoun
began to irritate me. Although a talented writer and
clearly conscious and critical of the two-tier class structure she saw in a newly independent Ireland, she was
unfortunately patronising too. Sometimes these stereotypes were complimentary – admiring the beautiful clear
skin of the people she met – but often she complained
about the damp, the living conditions, or spoke of Irish
evasiveness. Her musing on fairies and the supernatural
were not to my taste and she had an underlying desire
for Ireland not to modernise, but to stay as it was – a
wild playground for her to enjoy.

I felt I was not learning any more from her about the
lives of women on this coastline. But she did force me
to further confront my own romanticisation of Ireland's
'wildness'. After all, many of her preoccupations – of
swimming and walking, landscape and folklore – are
my own. The established conventions of holidaying
in Ireland that Edna O'Brien had written about in
Mother Ireland were exactly what I was doing as a
tourist. We walk, we swim, we eat and drink, visit holy
wells, comment on the local scenery and have a gener-
ally 'jolly' time. Except that leaving Roundstone, for
some reason, I wasn't. Constantly driving unfamiliar
roads and days of walking for three or four hours were
taking their toll and my faith in my entire enterprise

– of my intentions and capability – seemed to be dipping again. Ithell Colquhoun's dated point of view had brought me down. I continued on, stopping to swim at what I felt was perhaps the most beautiful beach of the entire coast, Glassilaun, where an English woman walking the strand took me into her confidence as I changed. She told me that her father had felt forced to leave in the 1940s, before showing me small cowrie shells she had found on the strand.

I realise now I was tired, and it was to be my undoing. With so much time in my own company, buried thoughts and experiences were coming to the surface. The history I was learning was almost too much to take in. Combined with the beauty of Connemara it was a sensory overload – I kept taking photographs on my phone but none of them could capture it, and I began to sketch more. I could not believe, in some ways, that Connemara existed – we must have driven through it many, many times as children on our annual journey between Limerick and Sligo but I could not recall it. How self-absorbed I must have been. What I did recall – inexplicably – was an Irish boyfriend that I'd had in my early thirties. I'd met him on a job while working as a documentary researcher and things had gone well. He'd been keen – almost too keen, I'd felt at the time – as well as kind and patient, but I'd pushed him away.

At Killary Fjord I'd sat and looked out at the rain hitting my windshield, pointlessly churning over what had, back then, seemed like a minor decision. He was Irish – had I been pushing away part of my Irishness? He wanted kids – he was very clear – had I been pushing that away too? As I ruminated, I realised that it wasn't even about him: it was about anxiety. Something that comes upon me whenever I am overwhelmed, faced with what I perceive as a big life decision or hard task. An indecision that creeps up on me when I am overdoing it – as I was at work back then, as I was on this road trip.

Outside Leenane, on a curve in the road, I lost control of the steering wheel and found myself in the ditch, with an extremely hardy gorse bush taking off the entire wing mirror and an embarrassingly big dent in the passenger front door. A man stopped and asked me if I was OK, reassured me that it happened all the time around these bends, that I wasn't the first or last. I made it to Killadoon, County Mayo, where Mary, who ran the bed and breakfast, made me tea while her husband got to work with some gaffer tape. But my spirit was broken. I headed back to Sligo and my parents' house and vowed that the following summer I would continue my journey.

I returned to my everyday life in London, surprised after my three months off how a level of restlessness I'd not noticed before underpinned the life of the city. Everybody seemed anxious – about work, about children, about house prices. Two of my friends – both still single like me, one in her fifties and the other my own age – announced that they were leaving London: the first to Hastings on the south coast of Britain, the second to Yorkshire to live closer to her sister. It was something to think about – whether my new-found joy in Ireland was something more permanent. I spent the weeks working in television again, enjoying the variety of freelance work that came my way, seeing my friends in the evenings at exhibitions or for swims in the lido. But I spent my weekends and my days off absorbing myself in Maude Delap's life or Peig

Sayers's stories. It was an interesting juxtaposition – my interior life was now vividly alive, yet most of my closest friends didn't know who any of the Irish women I was researching were, and so I began to feel almost like two people. At the archives of the Linnean Society, just off Piccadilly, I looked at little specimens of moss Ellen Hutchins had collected, preserved on two-hundred-year-old blotting paper. The specimens had 'suffered', I read in the curator's notes, 'from the slow penetration of London dust into the cabinets'.

Researching the lives of the women in this book was giving me purpose. I found that I no longer had whole weekends without plans because I was constantly preoccupied with researching and writing. I didn't want to go out and socialise to the extent I had before. Why lose the next morning when I had my own work to do? Sitting in my flat, I thought about the edges of Ireland – about the sea which I sometimes missed and the clifftops in which I had felt both completely isolated and completely safe. I began to appreciate these women as actual people who lived actual lives, deeply entrenched in their environments, and to know that a few books read or a few days walking in these places could never really scratch the surface.

My summer of spending time in nature was also beginning to change me. Walking on the Atlantic coast had naturally made me think more about our climate and about how we preserve it, and I tried to make small differences. I bought a bike – in part to preserve the fitness I had built up from so much walking, but also to lessen my own carbon footprint – and I gave up meat from Monday to Friday.

In truth, I missed Ireland – missed being more fully immersed in nature. I spent more time by the banks of the Thames walking, began swimming in the docks to feel part of London, of its moving river heart. Sometimes when I couldn't sleep I imagined myself back in that little cabin in Glengarriff, cradled by the sounds of the forest all around me.

But at last, now, I'm back on the road in Connemara, having decided after my brush with Ithell Colquhoun to focus my journey completely on women born in Ireland. To discover the work of a writer – Kate O'Brien, who, although born in Limerick, lived in Roundstone for ten years from 1950 to 1960. One of the most famous Irish female writers of her time, her novels – often set in her fictional version of Limerick, which she called Mellick – were once incredibly popular. As Dr Eibhear Walshe explains in his elegantly written biography *Kate O'Brien: A Writing Life*, for which I am grateful in my attempt to understand this complex woman, her novels broke the mould in her radical depiction of women as equal to men and sexually free. She was the first female Irish writer to write popular novels about Irish middle-class life. Her books often follow the same plot trajectory of a young woman who, leaving home and finding herself challenged by a moral quandary, decides to reject conformity and find her way towards independence in the world.

Kate O'Brien herself was a lesbian at a time when being so was barely acknowledged, and I am looking forward to her company because she strikes me as a true bohemian – someone who lived her life unapologetically, according to her own rules, in an era when it might have been difficult for her to do so. She is my guide for this length of coastline that she called 'my "own" south shore of Connemara' – a stretch of water along which she had, she said, 'left much of my heart'. Using her 1960 travelogue, *My Ireland*, as inspiration, I intend to walk through Roundstone village to Dog's Bay and Gurteen – two beaches on a tombolo that on my previous journey I experienced in overcast, foreboding weather. This time I'm hoping I will be luckier.

Kate O'Brien – the third O'Brien in this book, all of whom are from either Limerick or Clare – was born in 1897 into a fairly wealthy family. As her friend Lorna Reynolds wrote in her memoir *Kate O'Brien: A Literary Portrait*, her prosperous middle-class childhood in Limerick led her to expect others to be what she called 'agreeably civilised'. Her father was a successful horse dealer, full of charm and life, but there was also a streak of whimsy in the family – in a grand gesture, O'Brien's grandfather had named their house in tribute to former High King of Ireland Brian Boru. But her comfortable childhood was also marked with tragedy – she was just five years old when her mother, Katherine, died of cancer. Kate was sent to a nearby convent to be schooled by nuns – a situation she would idealise in her later book *The Land of Spices*. Many of her heroines would also be motherless.

O'Brien was one of life's wanderers, flitting periodically between different houses and flats in both England and Spain throughout her life, before spending her most settled years here in Galway. She had come to Roundstone in 1950 off the back of what was her greatest literary success – *That Lady*, a historical novel about a love triangle between wealthy Ana de Mendoza, Philip II of Spain and the king's secretary of state, set in the Spanish court at the end of the sixteenth century. Lorna Reynolds writes how, worried that O'Brien was recklessly wasting her newfound wealth, she advised her to invest in a property. O'Brien therefore came to Connemara full of hope. The war was over, and having spent the whole six years of it in London, a newly independent Ireland seemed appealing to a person who rarely stayed anywhere long.

She spent her ten years in this village in a house called The Fort, and as I walk along the lane into Roundstone, I know instinctively which house it is. On the edge of the village – a grey two-storey, built on a rock promontory that looks out onto the Atlantic Ocean, high walls all around it. As I pass, on the other side of the gate a dog barks loudly, sensing my presence. A former doctor's dispensary, it's a grand house, in which Kate O'Brien – with what the Belfast painter James MacIntyre described in 1951 as a menagerie of cats – lived in grand style, furnishing the house with exquisitely decorated ornate rugs, leather chairs and oil paintings. Many accounts exist of her extravagant hospitality, and Lorna Reynolds writes that it seems she was generous to the extreme, rarely turning anyone away, especially writers, and this made The Fort something of a destination for those travelling the west coast. O'Brien saw her house as a romantic place, definitely haunted – she said the villagers thought she had been mad to buy it and was brave to sleep there alone. In his book, Eibhear Walshe puts forward that she eventually fictionalised it as 'Glassala', the mysterious ancestral home of the Delahunts in her 1953 novel *The Flower of May*.

The owner of my bed and breakfast, Eileen, with whom I have formed an immediate bond, has arranged an introduction for me to the composer and his wife who now own it. When we discuss Kate's life here, they tell me that the ghost Kate O'Brien delighted in is still rumoured to haunt the upstairs room, where a woman can sometimes be seen reading at the window. In *My Ireland*, O'Brien advises that 'for Connemara especially it is true – more true than any part of Ireland – that all one needs for its discovery is a roadmap and a clear, mild day – in April, May, June, or in October or December'. I am here in August, ignoring her advice, but returning to Roundstone, full of the joy of being back on the road, is like visiting a friend. Last night I took it easy, walking from my bed and breakfast just outside the village into O'Dowd's for dinner, and walking back, as darkness fell, the light was extraordinary.

At the slipway down into the bay, boats are moored – mainly small fishing boats and a couple of dinghies. From here, if I look back, I can see how the promontory on which the house is built juts out into a crescent, on top of which sits the garden. Kate O'Brien wrote how on her walks – with her beloved cats – she would follow the morning star, waking at dawn to watch the sun rise over the Bens.

Kate O'Brien's books reflect her personality – they have a romantic touch but also contain an undercurrent of quiet rebellion that her readers must have identified with. They are often about forbidden or doomed love and violent passions – adultery, love between men and men, or women and women. Like Edna O'Brien who came after, her books were also banned in newly independent Ireland. Kate O'Brien's first book to be declared obscene in Ireland was *Mary Lavelle* (1936), in which the character of Agatha declared her love for the titular Mary, saying that she liked her in the same way a man would.

O'Brien seems to have initially tried to conform. In 1923, at the age of twenty-six, she had a brief failed marriage with a Dutch journalist called Gustaaf Renier, which Lorna Reynolds thought ended because of differing temperaments. Walshe puts forward that Renier was gay or bisexual himself, as well as having affairs with other women, and although unproven speculation, O'Brien was rumoured to have given birth to a child that might have been adopted by her sister. After this, O'Brien seems to have embraced her sexuality and had a series of female partners throughout her life. But by the time O'Brien moved to Roundstone, at the age of forty-seven, she was single and embracing the solitary life.

The coast road to the village follows a marshy shore full of dark brown and red seaweed. It begins to rain gently as I continue on towards the village main street, past the house of the late nature writer Tim Robinson and his wife, Mairéad, on the tip of the quay that faces The Fort, and in whose wanderings across the bogs this stretch of coastline has been so faithfully documented. Roundstone has always been an artistic hub, O'Brien writes in *My Ireland* – a place for naturalists and folklore collectors. 'Botanists and shell-gatherers and people who "derive" things from seaweed can find occupations all about; and as has been said, for scholars there is Gaelic; and folklore. There are birds too, seabirds, and swans and little furtive coots and such; snipe and plover crying, and wild geese.'

I stop for shelter from the cold rain in one of the pubs, a typical bar, now owned by a woman from Essex, not far from the London suburb in which I grew up, and we soon find ourselves in full flow. I order my umpteenth bowl of seafood chowder and another English couple, from Yorkshire this time, arrive so that the discussion opens further – where they've been, where I've been and where we are both headed next. They've been celebrity-spotting in Galway at the arts festival and list off the people they've seen, while I keep my own, rather niche obsessions to myself, aware they might think I am quite mad for using a 1960s travelogue as my guide. But then so what if I am, I think, as the conversation cools, and consider whether this is one of the bars in which O'Brien whiled away her ten years in Roundstone, firmly entrenched for the first time in Irish village life.

Eibhear Walshe cites an account he read by a writer called Val Mulkerns who, in 1951, stopped off at The Fort on a cycling tour of Connemara and noticed that, in the low-ceilinged pub, O'Brien had a found a place in the community, saying hello to everyone on the main street and buying sweets for the children. I met one of these children on my weekend in Roundstone – Christina Lowry, sitting in her conservatory at the back of the general store on the main street that smelt of fresh-baked bread. Christina told me she remembered Kate O'Brien as a woman who was ahead of her time, who loved to discuss politics. She remembered her distinctly, walking elegantly up the street wearing a beret and a cloak and carrying a stick. Although I have one account of O'Brien wearing a rustling black dress, most of the time she seems to have dressed in what would have then been called mannish clothes, as the portraits left behind of her show. Christina told me how much O'Brien loved children and would entertain them in the sunroom at The Fort.

Although she had grown up just two counties away, Kate O'Brien idealised Connemara and the villagers of Roundstone, whom she felt were austere and noble in bearing. 'Connemara,' she wrote, 'has a life very markedly its own, an elastic, quiet, unflurryable sort of life, which springs from the character of its inhabitants, but which after a time admits the pleasant stranger quite cordially to its habit.'

In *My Ireland*, she idealised Connemara as a pure place, where I feel that 1960s vices could not reach. In one passage she cautions any adventurous male readers that if they are thinking of getting lucky with a dewy-eyed colleen, they're in for a disappointment. She reports that Irish women are, on the whole, chaste and goes on, a few pages later, to recount a scene that she once observed in a bar in the West of Ireland, much like the one I am sitting in now, where a tourist flirted with one of the local barmaids only to be met with disdainful indifference.

My lunch complete, I walk uphill following the road that curves through the village, past a basketball court and the sign to Malachy's bodhrán shop, where a few tourists are out now that it's dry, sitting on the benches on the side of the road. As I leave the village, I notice Errisbeg is still covered in mist, even now as it nears 2 p.m. The road becomes dangerous for walking – cars come at me at 80 kilometres an hour and I have to keep my wits about me, pressing myself into the thistles and loosestrife that grow along the verges. The blackberries here in Roundstone are ripe and I nibble as I walk, enjoying the late-summer taste. What a view these houses built alongside the road must have on a clear day from their carefully tended lawns. I suddenly feel very cynical, as I wonder how much they must cost. It was obvious to me last night as I ate outside O'Dowds, looking at the people sitting on the wall drinking, that weekend homes and second homes, possibly bought by interlopers like myself, must make up a good proportion of the houses here, and Eileen back at the B&B had confirmed that it's the case. I wonder if this is simply the fate of somewhere so beautiful – in Kate O'Brien's time, she had written of the holidaymakers, of new bungalows springing up, but she had not complained. I suppose she was an incomer herself and had seen it as inevitable – an indication of change.

Between the fields is the dark wet ground of the bogs, strewn with the occasional large rock, in which tall reeds and stalks of dandelion grow. The day has warmed up and I pick up my pace. The black and white tarmacked road is freshly painted and it winds and curves in ever more perilous arcs. I begin to dread the corners, where I have to be extra alert, extra vigilant for the cars. At the top of one steep bend, I catch a glimpse of Gurteen falling beneath me to my left – the five bays, each covered in bright white sand. The Errisbeg peninsula is shaped like a bone, with Errisbeg mountain at one end and the headland jutting out into two points. On each side of the peninsula lies a beach – the first Gurteen and the second Dog's Bay. A sign in Irish tells me I am at Port na Feadóige, while in English it says simply 'Holiday Complex', after which the pre-fabs begin, the plots outside them overgrown. I turn left towards the faint sound of the sea, passing a holiday let where the garden has run rampant.

Gurteen is peopled with beach lovers, and I navigate around sunbathers and dog walkers, crossing each bay one by one until I reach the last – just the sea on my left and the bare sand-dunes to my right. On this, the longest beach, thong weed has been washed up in thin spaghetti-like strips. As the bay curves around, grass begins to grow on the dunes and little moon jellyfish appear on the shore line, hot-pink membranes glowing inside their bodies. I follow the path through the dunes to another small deserted cove where, among the shells and rocks, is ghostly white seaweed that I have never seen before – long strands of it, spread across the sand. I wonder if it has been bleached here by the sun.

I meet three Dubliners out with a dog, who advise me to take off my shoes for my walk across the top of the peninsula, where cattle are grazing on wet land. In minutes I realise that I have been given good advice – my walking boots would have been sodden otherwise. A rabbit hops across my path as I try not to walk into cattle fields – but the fences here seem anarchic and are often torn down by the wind, and so my trail is mostly guesswork. At a certain point a large boggy pond means I can go no further, but no matter because I'm already at the tip of the sand spit that makes up the end of the tombolo – the two beaches of Gurteen and Dog's Bay at either side beneath me. It's half past three now, two hours since I left Roundstone. I leave Gurteen behind me, crossing the headland towards the beach of Dog's Bay. The wind picks up and I can hear the distinctive high-pitched sound of children playing.

O'Brien speaks in *My Ireland* of how these beaches are a place for children, and she clearly enjoyed their company. She clung to her own childhood throughout her life. Her great heroine was Saint Teresa of Ávila, a sixteenth-century Spanish noblewoman who had also lost her mother when she was still a child. Being called to a religious life, Saint Teresa experienced 'raptures' in which she spoke to God, sometimes levitating, and was known to have reformed the Carmelite order of nuns. O'Brien never lost her own reverence for the nuns who had taught her from the age of six, and her aunts had also entered the Presentation convent in Limerick. Combined, these women and their world of sisterly camaraderie and competition became important female influences for a little girl lacking a mother. In one of her most engrossing novels, 1941's *The Land of Spices*, the main character, Anna Murphy, is sent to a convent boarding school when very young. Anna has a female mentor in the form of the convent's reverend mother. Without giving away too much, the novel was banned in Ireland for one crucial line, where the heroine discovers that her father has a secret that she cannot quite accept.

The stability of convent life – of places where women work together in security and solidarity – appealed to O'Brien, but looking at her life as a whole, she herself was very much an outlier, flitting between homes and partnerships throughout. She's a slippery character, with whom on the surface I feel I have a lot in common. I went to a convent – a day school in East London – as a child; my mother is from a middle-class Limerick family, although not as grand as O'Brien's; she spent much of her career in London and even worked, as I have done, for the BBC. But for some reason, Kate O'Brien still feels difficult for me to understand. And the more I read, the more I wonder if she knew this about herself – that she was in some way impenetrable? As Eibhear Walshe points out in his biography, she often changed small details about her life in interviews – making herself younger, for example.

In *My Ireland*, there is a passage in which she is speaking about her life in Connemara and a visit to the fair on Omey Island, which is just a little along the coast from Roundstone and Dog's Bay. The fair at Omey sparks a memory of the sideshows of Duffy's Circus in Kilkee when she was a child.

> My favourite was Find the Lady, the Three Card Trick. I lost much copper and small silver in adolescence, in pursuit of the Queen of Spades. I had forgotten it, the mystery, the speed, how many faces of tricksters and dupes – until I heard the cry again at the races at Omey – Find the Lady! It was a great and peaceful pleasure to pause and look for her once more, in vain … simply I had liked the hiddenness of her in the three cards, I liked being fooled.

I feel I have been playing this game with Kate O'Brien. At every turn, I find her both refreshing and contradictory – sometimes she is caught up in middle-class manners; sometimes she is a bold individualist. O'Brien believed that women should be free to follow their own destinies – exemplified by her female protagonists as well as her many relationships with other women. Yet, she also revered the staunch Catholicism in which she had been raised. My only reliable foothold on her life seems to be in her books and here in the landscape of Connemara, on this path that I know she walked too. I round the corner, still hearing the sound of the children on the beach but I cannot yet see them, and I wonder if the wind is playing tricks on me. I begin to think that I have vastly underestimated the length of this walk. But then, all at once, the spectacular horseshoe shape of Dog's Bay with its more-than-a-mile-long stretch of white sand appears beneath me. I come across a large black and green beetle in difficulty on his back and tip him over. Soon my bare feet are walking on soft white sand.

O'Brien's friends appear to have seen her ten years in Roundstone as something of a mistake – the start of what would become a descent into alcoholism. Her lifelong confidante Lorna Reynolds came to regret advising O'Brien to buy a house in Connemara. She felt it was too isolated and it was too easy for O'Brien to fall into the habit of drinking. O'Brien had spent much of her working life in London, and although she loved village life, she found herself missing the company of other writers, surrounded as she was by holidaymakers and fishermen.

By the late fifties, despite still having plenty of journalistic work, O'Brien was being forced to borrow money. But she was still forthright and bold. In her final completed novel, *As Music and Splendour*, the two female characters, for the first time in her novels, have their own careers. By 1958, O'Brien found herself penniless – a victim of her own largesse. By 1960, she had sold The Fort and moved to Ávila in Spain in an attempt live more cheaply. The last fourteen years of her life would be difficult. As a freelance writer, she had rarely saved and had no pension and no support other than that of her wealthy sister Nance O'Mara, who eventually settled her in a cottage in Kent. She continued to write a column for *The Irish Times* but would never complete another novel.

The end of Kate O'Brien's life was a solitary one. But I do not find her the sorry, lonely person her friends may have thought she was – perhaps a little melancholy at times, as she got older, but isn't that only natural for someone who had lived such a full life in her youth? For me, O'Brien's mishandling of her money as a freelancer is something I see as a salutary tale, as is the depressive effect of alcohol on an already restless mind. Her drinking made me examine my own relationship with booze and of course the thought naturally occurred – as other single friends left London – could I be happy living here in this beautiful part of the West of Ireland?

Roundstone suited Kate O'Brien in part – the small community of the village at that time clearly welcomed and enjoyed her. I think she herself must have known that the issue with having moved to Roundstone was that she had no intimate companions here, whether friends or lovers, and she drowned those sorrows rather than addressed them. Ireland is obviously different now from how it was in those post-war years – there are creative communities all along this coastline. I'm meeting people I feel could become friends as I go: a second-generation musician swimming at Blackrock in Galway just a few days back had told me she didn't regret her move; a midwife-turned-hotel-owner in Lahinch had trained in England and still missed it sometimes, she said. People move back and forth all the time – it's part of the ebb and flow between our countries. But the idea of moving permanently is daunting.

On the beach at Dog's Bay, I realise that I've made a wrong call in terms of the swim I've been craving – the water here is too shallow for anything but a dip, and the beach is too windswept to really enjoy. I continue on, back up to the main road, until I am retracing my own steps to Gurteen, taking my wetsuit out of my rucksack on an area of the beach overlooked by a neatly kept graveyard. As I swim I think about O'Brien's life, how her friends felt her years in Connemara were a mistake. But Walshe begins his chapter on Kate O'Brien's time in Connemara by citing a radio interview with RTÉ in 1973, in which O'Brien calls her time in Roundstone as having been in 'Lotus Land'. The name refers to one of the books in Homer's *Odyssey* in which he and his shipmates encounter a group of islanders who are addicted to a mysterious plant – possibly opium – that induces complete and blissful oblivion.

Despite the heavy drinking, O'Brien worked steadily while she lived at the Fort, producing two novels and two biographies as well as countless articles and short stories. Although she bemoaned not having other intellectuals around her, to me it seems that she was in some way happy here. Happy enough to write that:

> on a little hill of Gurteen Beach, at an angle before it curves into Dog's Bay, there is a graveyard where the Roundstone people are buried; and I used to say that one reason why I lived in Roundstone was to have the pleasure of being buried there. This will not happen now, so where the tree falls let it lie, in Heaven's name.

She goes on to say that the best black sole in Europe are caught in these waters below the graveyard, in the shadow of which, I realise later, I had been swimming. In the end, she died in a hospital in Kent, alone at the age of seventy-six, on 13 August 1974, and she is buried there, where her tombstone simply reads: 'Pray for the wanderer'.

Kate O'Brien was a natural wanderer, I think, instinctively following where life led her. She also liked risk – was someone who loved a harmless gamble. She'd written her first play in London, back in 1925, as the result of a bet with her friend Veronica Turleigh, a UCD graduate like herself. Moving to Roundstone was a risk, but sometimes you have to take risks, don't you?

It was an incredibly brave move for Kate O'Brien to implant herself, as a single woman, into a community. I wonder if she hadn't drunk so much, hadn't entertained so much, hadn't ultimately run out of money, perhaps she would not have been so alone in her later years? Could she have continued to live in Roundstone, enjoying her home as a bohemian outpost for those passing through? Throughout her life, she never really settled in a place that she could call home, wandering as the mood took her. This worked in her early days when she had close relationships, but home is people rather than places too, I reflect – and finding the right person is, of course, hard. I park the thought for now. Where and how I spend the rest of my life is not something that's going to work itself out in an afternoon.

Despite, or maybe because of, her enigmatic personality, Kate O'Brien has excited me about my journey again, made me happy to wander a little more. I am two-thirds up the coastline now and about to travel backwards in time into parts of Irish history I know very little about – into the life of two great queens of Irish history: first my namesake Grace O'Malley, or Gráinne Ní Mháille, whose legend I have been preoccupied with since I was a child, and afterwards Queen Maeve, an ancient queen of Connacht, buried not far from my parents' house in County Sligo.

9. QUEEN OF CLEW BAY

Granuaile
Clare Island, County Mayo

Up past the fjord of Killary, I travel through Leenane, coming into conversation with my past self as I look for the place of my car accident two years ago, where, although the day was beautiful and the scenery superlative, somehow my brain and body had conspired against me. I know now that I'd hit the brakes too suddenly on that corner, that I was taking it too wide and too fast. I'm embarrassed but also proud of myself that I'm used to driving in Ireland now, that it is becoming more familiar. I also realise as I pass that it doesn't really matter, that time has moved on and I am no longer the person I was, that I trust myself a little more than I once did. I am ready, I think, for my next walk: on the island home of Gráinne Ní Mháille – a fierce woman with no time for any kind of internal hand-wringing – who sailed these shores four hundred years ago and with whom I share my name. As with many of the women in this book, I'm conflicted as to what to call her. Should I use her first name or her surname? Her English or Irish name? In the end I take my lead from author Anne Chambers, whose definitive biography, *Grace O'Malley: The Biography of Ireland's Pirate Queen, 1530–1603*, I used as my guide, calling her Granuaile.

Growing up, Granuaile was often mentioned in our house as my parents tried to help me to enjoy, to be proud of a name which in London, with every new school year and new round of pronunciation explanations, was fast becoming tiresome. She is known now as a 'pirate queen', a clan leader in sixteenth-century Ireland who ruled the waters around Mayo's Clew Bay, taxing and plundering as she went and defending a territory her family had held for generations. As a child, I thought of her in the same way I might think of Robin Hood – as an almost mythic, unreal figure, as I supposed all pirates were.

As I started out on my journey into the life of this woman I have heard so much about, I was surprised to find that, rather than a myth, she is very much a historical figure, rescued from historical obscurity by Anne Chambers and her late 1970s research into the Elizabethan State Papers and other contemporary sources, piecing together for the first time Granuaile's life, to which I am indebted. The daughter of a Gaelic chieftain, Granuaile, I found out, was a canny politician who navigated the Tudor invasion of Ireland in a way that suited her family's interests. I was also surprised to learn that her deeds are not recorded in the Irish annals – the records that various Irish monks and scholars kept of their history – so almost every historical fact we know about Granuaile comes from records kept by the English Tudor court that were first deciphered by Chambers.

What I find astounding about Granuaile is the strength of her myth – a place at table is still laid for her at Howth Castle, where legend has it she was once refused entry and so responded by abducting the heir. Tales abound of the incredible feats she accomplished sailing the stormy seas around this coast and the true joy of her story comes from this folklore, embellished across the centuries, as part of the Irish oral storytelling tradition. In these tales she was an enthusiastic gambler, was sexually liberated and often took lovers. I cringe a little to admit it, but as an English child who was constantly having to explain my name, I secretly clung to Granuaile and her legend. I liked that she was wild and free, that she could do what the boys did and that nothing, seemingly, could stop her.

Early on a Monday morning I take a ferry from Roonagh Pier out to Clare Island, my only companions two workmen who load up their equipment before sitting silently at the other end of the boat. The ferry is fast and we're there in under twenty minutes. My intention today is to do my toughest walk yet, circling the island via its highest point – Knockmore, at 462 metres. From there I'll hopefully have a vantage-point of a good part of Granuaile's territory, which stretched across Clew Bay. She was the only child of chieftain Owen Dubhdara, or 'black oak', Uí Máille, a hereditary lord. Anne Chambers explains how the fort at Clare Island was one of five castles the O'Malleys had built in and around Clew Bay. Chambers also writes that, as a child, Gráinne probably divided her time between here and the family's principle home of Belclare. She was learning from her father and his followers how to navigate the Atlantic weather systems and the tides. Folklore says that at twelve years old, desperate to go to sea with her father, he tried to put her off with the warning that her long hair would get caught in the sails. Determined, she cut off her hair and was nicknamed Gráinne Mhaol – which means 'Gráinne the bald'.

Clare Island is the most mountainous of all the islands in Clew Bay, and I feel that the walk up to Knockmore will reflect Granuaile's own tenacious character. Although it is by no means the highest of Ireland's mountains, for me it will be a big achievement and I'm interested to see if I can do it. The walk starts by the harbour, where Granuaile's Clare Island fortress survives, and will take me by the lighthouse over the peak of Knockmore and then to the other side of the island where the queen is buried. As Anne Chambers notes, Granuaile lived here from roughly 1560–67, after the death of her first husband – a rash and aggressive chieftain called Dónal-an-Chogaidh, whom she'd married when she was just sixteen. With Dónal she had two sons, Owen and Murrough, as well as a daughter called Margaret, and by the time of his death, she was in her early thirties.

The newly widowed Granuaile came here to Clare Island, bringing with her those men who had remained loyal to her. With three galleys and a fleet of smaller boats, she protected her own territory – sometimes trading with, sometimes taxing and sometimes plundering ships she encountered on the Atlantic waves as she dominated the sea around Clew Bay. In an age before accurate maps, Granuaile's local knowledge and experience of this unpredictable coastline made it possible, in these years of her life, to live as she wished.

From the clifftop on which the fortress is built, it's possible to see all passing traffic in the bay. I walk around the tall, blocky building, built with thin, high windows to protect against the wind. Through the metal bars are the remains of what were three storeys connected by a staircase, with fireplaces and chimneys on each floor. To me, it seems tiny inside, but in Granuaile's time it would have dwarfed any other dwellings on this island, a clear sign to any passing ships just who was in charge. The house would have been heated by fires and the upper floors hung with animal skins and decorated with furniture or rugs acquired as a result of trade or raids. Beneath the tower lies another sheltered beach, slightly away from the island's main strand and hidden unless you go looking – perfect for swimming or smuggling – which I eye up as a place to pass an hour or so later, if I can make good time on my hike.

From the tower, I follow the road that runs parallel to the island's main beach where, in front of the community centre, I take a left through an area of the island called Faunglass. Knocknaveen, the smaller of Clare Island's two mountains, looms over me on my left as I pass through two wooden gates guarded by a flock of horned Mayo sheep, each marked with a pink 'H'. They stand up as I approach, move when I walk and stop when I stop, so that soon I am herding fifteen or so sheep along a lane, bleating against my intrusion. The landscape is now bare and treeless, the path an upwards incline, and my only company the now docile sheep who watch my progress through this part of the island, which my map tells me is called Maum. As I walk the eastern coastline, I can see what I think must be the large circular cages of salmon farms out on the ocean surface, a line of vapour on the water behind them.

I pass a clutch of weathered tree stumps on either side of the road – the remnants of an ancient Scot's pine forest, preserved by the acidity of the bog and possibly felled, I read, by the island's earliest inhabitants around 7,500 years ago. The ground is soft and springy underneath me as I veer off the path to look more closely at these fossils of another age – the bark cracked and splintered, coloured ash grey by time, the circles on the tree trunks incredibly detailed. Sometimes the wood has shattered into sharp pieces that are scattered across the ground like a ghost forest on this black bog. A flock of starlings lift off nearby, making a noise like the wind every time they arc and resettle on another bank, or sometimes on the electricity cables, where they sit in three neat rows. I look up and see the cause of their trouble – a peregrine falcon, soaring above me out to the east. The withered stumps of the ancient forest continue along the sides of the path as the road begins to slope downwards. Knockmore, in front of me, where I am headed, is still cloaked in white.

In 1565, as I learnt from Anne Chambers's biography, when Granuaile was living on Clare Island as a widow, Ireland was a politically volatile place to live. Interclan rivalry between chiefs was common, as were wars between the hereditary peers and landowners that had emerged as a result of previous British invasions. Concerns about Philip II of Spain using Catholic Ireland as a base to attack England were growing. The solution, as the English saw it, was colonisation – settling the sons of the English landed gentry in Ireland. As Ireland became more and more unstable, Granuaile decided, in 1567, when she was thirty-seven, to get married again – to Richard-an-Iarainn Bourke, a chieftain who was eligible to inherit an important title: the MacWilliamship. Folklore has it that Granuaile insisted on a trial marriage of one year – which was common among the Irish aristocracy – perhaps to ensure he was not as hot-headed as her first husband.

In the end, she and Richard were a good match – a sixteenth-century power couple who had a son together, Tibbot-na-Long, which in English means 'Toby of the Ships', supposedly called as he was born aboard ship. Legend has it, as recounted by Chambers, that the day after his birth Granuaile's ship was attacked by Algerian pirates and, in despair, the captain asked her to come aboard deck. She is said to have responded, 'May you be seven times worse off this day [for] twelve months, who cannot do without me for one day' – a story that amplifies her almost superhuman powers.

I reach a place where three roads meet. One leads straight to my destination – the Cistercian Abbey in which Granuaile is buried – but I am going the long way round. I cross another cattle grid where the land becomes track, and now Knockmore appears to my left, like a giant nose on the landscape. The lighthouse is before me in the distance on a road that is steadily rising in steepness. Through the boggy fields at either side of me, covered in purple heather, streams of water trickle towards the eastern shore. Clare Island lighthouse is now a luxury hotel, or so I was told by my bed and breakfast hosts in Westport, and I meet a van coming from it on the road, no doubt on the way to pick up guests coming in on the late-morning ferry. In the distance, I hear a sound like a water pump out there in the bay and look out to see a boat on the horizon.

By her mid-thirties Granuaile had already established a fearsome reputation as both a sailor and ruler. Over the course of her lifetime, men such as Sir Francis Drake and Sir Walter Raleigh were on the up – making their fortunes plundering and colonising the new world. The idea to them, and indeed perhaps to her Irish contemporaries, that a woman could captain a ship would have been odd in the extreme. Sir Henry Sidney, the then Lord Secretary of Ireland, met Granuaile and Richard in Galway City in 1577, when she was forty-seven, recounting the meeting in a letter to Francis Walsingham in 1583, now held in the National Archives at Kew in West London. Led there by Anne Chambers's work, I found myself fascinated by his description of 'Grany Imallye', a woman 'notorious in all the coasts of Ireland', and her offer to him of three galleys and two hundred fighting men.

The tales of her marauding and fighting are incredible. Chambers writes that supposedly, whenever visiting Inishbofin, she would run an iron chain across the harbour to prevent access to the island and once launched a cannonball at Curragh Castle in Renvyle. In the midst of battle at Kinturk Castle, she is said to have reprimanded her own son, Tibbot-na-Long, saying, 'Are you trying to hide behind my backside, the place you came from?' It's an interesting story if true, Granuaile's use of humiliation as a motivator in battle, in a way that really only a mother could.

At the double-towered lighthouse, I sit down for a moment to catch my breath before I start the slow climb up along the slippery cropped grass of the clifftop, stopping every now and then to look back at the black and green cliffs falling beneath me. Out in front of me Achill Island is blanketed in cloud, while up to my right in the distance I can see my destination – the peak of Knockmore. Up here at the start of the mountainside, the grass beneath my feet is spongy and almost shockingly green. I come across a miniature clifftop pool with a still, glassy surface, like a portal to another world, about two metres across. It is eerie and black, this pool, reflecting the white disk of the sun as it tries to break through the gaps in the clouds. I wonder how deep it is. When I look back, the peregrine falcon I saw earlier is flying overhead, or perhaps it is a different bird. They are not territorial outside their nests, unlike human beings.

The more I read of Granuaile's life, and the more formidable she becomes in my mind, the more I see why her legend has survived – her character as clear as water.

By her fifties, however, her fortunes were sliding. Her husband had died, leaving her no inheritance, and she had a problem: the appointment of a brutal soldier called Sir Richard Bingham as governor of Connacht. He was to become her sworn enemy – a thorn in her side across the last two decades of her life, as Bingham sought to curtail her power.

I continue my way up the cliffs, crossing a stone stile, Knockmore always in the distance ahead of me. The grass has become an uneven surface, small tussocks of turf and heather where I must watch my footing, and although I keep a good safe distance from the cliff edge, at times the trail is open to the sharp drop to my right. Slipping along like this, I'm encouraged to see in front of me a horse treading a path upwards alongside another glassy cliff pool. I follow it up, crossing out of the farmland through a wire fence along a track where thistles graze my shins. Now I begin my ascent, climbing up the stepped banks. I foolishly try – for a good ten minutes at least – to continue along the rocky shore path, but with the cliffs becoming higher it is impassable, and there's now an added pressure. I can see, in the distance, another lone hiker making their way across the fields behind me, surely laughing at the unnecessary energy I've expended. Admitting defeat, I take a trail through the grassy hills instead, and after my moment of madness it seems childishly easy.

Until, that is, I reach the next hill. And it begins to dawn on me what I have taken on – an arduous hike across a series of hills until I reach the top of Knockmore. I trek up and then down, resting as I go because, unexpectedly, I have also got my period and it's a bad one. I haven't brought painkillers and I am annoyed with myself. I begin to think Granuaile was made of actual steel, that all the women of the past whose lives I have explored must have been people of extraordinary mettle.

It's nearing noon and I stop to eat lunch, letting the lone hiker I spotted earlier overtake me. I'm a little relieved to see that it's another woman. Her name is Ciara and she arrived on the ferry just after my own, meaning she's made better time than I have. She stopped at the lighthouse but couldn't go in. 'It's all couples staying there,' she tells me. We agree it must be a honeymooning sort of place.

It occurs to me as we talk that Ciara is a more experienced walker than me. 'They're sea cliffs, really,' she says, then rather dauntingly tells me that we're as yet only 177 metres above sea level. 'It's deceptive,' she says, 'it's up and down all the way. But you're close.'

'Did you see my scramble earlier?' I ask her.

'I did. I thought to myself, I don't fancy that.'

I tell Ciara that I'm finding it tough, and I must look exhausted because she offers to stay with me but I let her go on.

'Just follow the sheep trails,' she says, then continues on her way.

Although widowed a second time, Granuaile still had her skills as a marauder, and there was additional opportunity for plunder, as the next year, in the summer of 1588, having failed to invade England, twenty-six galleons and gunships of Phillip II's Spanish Armada were pushed by storms along the west coast of Ireland. But with the British now more aggressive than ever, Granuaile's life was again under surveillance, as Bingham began to move ever closer to complete domination – in 1592, Chambers notes, for the first time, he parked his warships in Clew Bay.

Over the next hour, the views of the bay – in which I now can imagine every kind of sixteenth-century ship, from Granuaile's galleys to Spanish galleons and Bingham's warships – become more spectacular as the walking gets tougher. Having at first delighted in my isolation on this clifftop, as with each step I become more weary, I'm increasingly grateful to know that my fellow walker Ciara is here, albeit a substantial amount of steps ahead of me. When I finally reach the summit – marked by a small square concrete monument covered in midges – I see Ciara sitting outside a large, thankfully midge-free stone cairn across the way and I join her as she eats her lunch. She works in engineering, she tells me, and is here for a weekend's walking on her own.

As I suspected, she's a much more seasoned hiker than me. I tell her that the only climb I've found tougher in Ireland is Croagh Patrick – Ireland's most famous pilgrim trail – in Mayo, which is not for the faint-hearted. It was so arduous I used a wooden walking stick to make my way up it.

'And you know the worst thing about that is that Croagh Patrick is most people's only experience of hiking, and it's awful – it's just scree. And once they do it, they never want to go hiking in Ireland again,' she says. We are soon deep in conversation about whether or not we feel we could live on a small island such as this – whether it is safer in smaller communities, whether it is safe to walk like this, in isolated places on our own. She confides that she was also pleased to see that I was a woman.

We admire the views sitting there together – of Inishturk, Inishbofin and the hazy blue outline of Achill, covered in clouds – until Ciara is ready to go. 'Don't try to keep up following me down,' she says, 'because I've been told I'm very fast descending.' I eventually get moving too, heading down the south-western plateau of the island, the endless propelling forward almost as tough as the climb. Ciara was right – she's flown it and is nowhere to be seen, while I sit down to rest occasionally as my stomach cramps, my body heavy with relief each time I do. It's a warm day now and I'm beginning to feel the exhilaration of having completed the climb. I head down towards the road to the abbey, to the grave of the woman who once ruled this island.

The most famous tale about Granuaile is of her meeting with Queen Elizabeth I in July 1593. Chambers writes of how Bingham had captured her favourite son, Tibbot, and so Granuaile decided to do something about her situation, for once and for all, by appealing to the highest authority she could. She first wrote to Elizabeth that summer, in a letter first deciphered by Chambers and which, when I saw it onscreen at the Kew Archives, where it has been scanned in high resolution, I found unexpectedly moving. In it she calls herself 'your loyall and faithful subject Grany ny Mally of Conaght in your highness realm of Ireland'. She outlined how over the years she had been forced to protect herself and went on to explain that, by Gaelic law, as a widow she had not been entitled to any provision to live upon. Granuaile was sixty-three by this time, and she asked for a royal patent in return for a surrender of her two sons' lands, as well as some provision – a pension of sorts – so that she could live out a peaceful old age.

Granuaile prostrates herself as a loyal subject, promising to vanquish Elizabeth's enemies, signing off that she will 'pray continually for your Majesties long life and prosperous reygne'. Following this letter, Granuaile went to London to meet Elizabeth from June until September 1593, and it's exciting for me to imagine her there. Tradition has it that she sailed there herself, and to the east of the city, on the banks of the Thames around Shadwell, Limehouse, Poplar or Rotherhithe – areas I know well, having lived in Limehouse for several years in my late twenties. When Granuaile visited, London was one of the greatest metropolises the world had ever seen – a place where the template for today's global cities was being laid down. Goods were being imported and exported from across the world – whether silk or opium, spices or sugar – and cargo ships were arriving daily as European powers colonised much of the globe.

Granuaile was granted an audience that July with Elizabeth. Folklore has it that it took place at the palace in Greenwich, now south-east London, on the site of what is today the Royal Naval College, in what was then the countryside. Elizabeth's father, Henry VIII, was born in Greenwich Palace, as was Elizabeth herself to Anne Boleyn, and as this was the palace where her mother was first presented as queen, it's possibly somewhere that she had special affection for. For me, Greenwich as a place is forever associated with Elizabeth, with trade and with ships. It's also somewhere I enjoyed visiting as a child with my father on half-terms and holidays – to see the tall ships race as it passed down river and take the river-bus into the city. I vividly remember going to see the Armada exhibition at the maritime museum and standing in front of the *Armada Portrait*, in which Elizabeth, in all her sumptuous finery, lays her hand on the globe. However more complicated my feelings might be now, having learnt a bit more history, nine-year-old me was beyond impressed.

I'm sure that Granuaile would have been too. Elizabeth dressed for maximum effect, with over two thousand dresses in her wardrobe, perhaps to distract from her black teeth and smallpox-marked skin. It is said that she covered her skin in Venetian ceruse – a paint made of white lead and vinegar, which was in itself corrosive. The two women were almost the same age when they met – Elizabeth I was sixty, just three years younger. She had never married and had no children, knowing, perhaps from what had happened to her father's many wives, that the only way to stay secure as a female leader was to make no alliance at all. Men could not be trusted. Granuaile, by contrast, had lived a much more adventurous, independent life. She had married twice and had several children. Yet in the end, her security depended on the decision of another woman. It's a fascinating encounter, perhaps because in history it is a rarity to have two powerful women beside each other like that.

Looking at these Tudor documents, they feel familiar to me – because I learnt Tudor history at school, I have the Elizabethan court in my head already. But now I'm finding out the other side – that Granuaile had been pushed into acquiescing to Elizabeth to preserve herself and her family. One story has it that Granuaile went barefoot to court – an account again from the wonderful Dúchas schools archive, from a County Mayo copybook collected some time in the 1930s, which states that Granuaile was outspoken, declined the present of a lapdog and dismissed a speech Elizabeth made about the cares of royalty, saying that the women of Mayo had more cares and were more industrious. The account ends with Granuaile declining the title of countess, as she is herself a queen. It shows the absolute power of Granuaile's myth. In reality, her position was much more precarious. Elizabeth does seem to have respected Granuaile, however – she granted her everything she asked for. As Anne Chambers again points out, Granuaile also made an impression at court – at the time she was in London, the Italian cartographer

Giovanni Battista Baozio was drawing his 1599 map of Ireland, in which her name features as the holder of territory across Clew Bay. Granuaile, for the time being, had won.

I follow the path of the river as it runs its way down the hillside, the riverbed the same dark peaty brown of the clifftop lakes, stones glowing like copper under the surface of the water. I pass by a pen full of sheep, hear the faint sound of a radio emanating from a farmhouse on the road beneath me. Back on a main road, I follow it round until I reach the village and then make my way to the Cistercian abbey, originally built by the O'Malleys in 1224, although the church that survives now is late medieval.

'There's no hurry,' says a woman at the black wooden door, carrying a key. 'Take as long as you want!' It is a dark place, where cardboard displays tell the story of the island. Granuaile is buried in the nave, underneath patches of medieval fresco left on the ceiling – the remains of red dragons, men on horseback, birds and trees. The tomb is inset into the left wall, beside which hangs, cut into the limestone, the O'Malley coat of arms – a galley with sail and five oars. Above it, the family motto: *terra marique potens* – 'powerful by land and sea'.

Sadly, Granuaile's victory had been short-lived, and she was forced to chase the pension she had been promised from Elizabeth. No response is recorded, so we don't know how she spent her last days. In 1603 – the same year Tibbot was knighted by James I – Granuaile passed away at the age of seventy-two or seventy-three. Here in the church, someone has left a flower on the grave – a single fake yellow rose made of fabric. I thought I would be emotional here in front of her grave. That I would feel moved to be in the same space as this formidable woman who once meant so much to me. But now I have researched her story properly, I seem to have lost some of my sentimentality for Granuaile and what I actually feel is a kind of terrified respect.

This was a person who clearly, beset on all sides by war, survived through being absolutely ruthless – someone with an incredible core of self-belief that few people are born with. Perhaps that's why I liked her so much as a child: she was proof that Gráinnes take no prisoners, are proud of themselves even if teachers and classmates think that their name is complicated and weird. I liked her vital unstoppability, that she was queen, captain, mother, raider, politician and wife all at the same time. But unlike the other women I have followed, she is also part myth, and now that I know more about how hard people's lives often were across the centuries on this west coast, I wonder if she is so loved and remembered because people needed a larger-than-life heroine like that? A woman who always sprang back up, whatever life threw at her? Who could not be defeated?

I'm proud of myself today. I'm sure for experienced climbers Knockmore is not a huge achievement – but for me, with these cramps and heavy bleeding, it has been a test. As I leave the abbey, I am full of the joy of having completed a long-held mission. I start the three-kilometre walk back to the quayside, stopping into a shop for a box of paracetamol and a celebratory ice cream. The shopkeeper discusses my route with me. I show him the way I went on the map sellotaped to the counter. 'That way you went is like walking up and down a Toblerone,' he says, but I also feel from him a new respect. His description is so accurate I wish I could share it with Ciara, but she has vanished, no doubt already on the ferry back and planning her next big walk.

I fill my water bottle from a pipe of spring water running down from the mountain – a notice telling me it's at my own risk – and continue around the south-eastern edge of the island. The road is closed to traffic today, and as I walk I see why. Three men are cutting back the hedgerows – an end-of-summer job. As I approach, one of the men mouths something to me over the noise, and as I pass, he stops and presents me with a gift – a stem of purple loosestrife. I feel sincerely loved, I tell him, and in truth, his joking around does pick me up, giving me the energy I need to get back to the quay. My feet are hurting now, and as the road widens I begin to fantasise about taking off my walking boots and getting into the sea, about the big soft bed at my parents' house in Sligo waiting for me when I return tomorrow. I've pushed my body today and it's made me contemplate even more what it might have been like for women centuries ago, without pain relief or contraceptives, and how much I take these things for granted. I can't stop thinking about Granuaile going into battle despite having just given birth, how it feels like a tall tale spun around some small kernel of truth.

Is this what happens to stories as time passes, I wonder? The few women who are remembered evolve into larger-than-life symbols of strength for the rest of us – people that we recollect and check in with when we're feeling a little unsteady? Today, Granuaile has helped me muster inner reserves I did not know I had. But still, I am happy to be heading back to my parents' home in Sligo tomorrow – to a bath, a duvet, my hot-water bottle and all my other twenty-first-century comforts.

10. MAEVE'S CAIRN

Queen Maeve of Connacht
Knocknarea, County Sligo

My mother thinks that all this gadding about the country is wearing me out and is encouraging rest – to spend drizzly mornings in bed with cups of tea, watch repeats on television, do the crossword with my dad and pick blackberries on the lane outside the house. Having now seen me, earlier in the summer, swimming enthusiastically at Rosses Point, my mum, who cannot swim herself, has decided to try to mitigate any more danger, buying me a neon tow float, a bright orange swim cap and a new Dryrobe. It's mid-September now, and I'm allowing myself two more weeks before I return to London and hustle for work. The unpredictable weather has turned again and now it's hot, perhaps the last hot day of the year, as I climb the path up to Miosgán Meadhbha – Queen Maeve's Cairn.

Of all the women in this book, Maeve is the one with whom I feel closest. Partly, this is geography – the cairn in which she is supposedly buried is just a twenty-five-minute drive from my parents' house. It sits, like an upside-down bowl, on the top of Knocknarea, a mountain next to the village of Strandhill, just outside Sligo town. The cairn is a mark on the landscape that anyone who has ever driven into Sligo from the west will know is impossible to miss, and this walk up Knocknarea to Maeve's grave is one I have done more often than any other in this book, reflecting not only her close proximity to my father's homeplace but also my love of ancient history and mythology. Aside from geography, the other reason I feel close to Maeve is that whenever I see her tomb as I drive along the N4 into Sligo town, it gives me a feeling I can't quite find the word for – a feeling of being connected, by landscape, to the people of the very ancient past. Of being part of a continuous story – a sort of *oh yes, I'm in all this too.*

Maeve, if she existed, was an Iron Age queen who lived around 50 CE and ruled from her palace at Rathcroghan in Roscommon. Her burial mound is, tradition has it, this ancient passage tomb on top of Knocknarea, although the tomb is much older than Maeve's legend. It was built around 3300 or 3400 BCE – the late Stone Age – and it is as much a part of Sligo's landscape as the great towering mountain of Benbulben. The people of Sligo love Queen Maeve's cairn, as do I – it is a marker and indication of pride in this county's landscape.

Maeve shares with Granuaile the reputation of a warrior queen – a fierce, indomitable matriarch. Reputedly married five times and buried upright to face her enemies, she was the ruler of Connacht in Irish mythology. The hike up to her grave is probably one of the most trodden paths of this book aside, of course, from the Cliffs of Moher, and

I have completed it at least four times that I can remember. Once with my dad, back when his legs would take him, twice on my own and once with my oldest friend, on a weekend visit from London earlier this summer. The only Irish walk I think I have done more in my life is to the large passage tombs from around the same period at Carrowkeel, hidden in the Bricklieve mountains.

Those ancient tombs, along with those at Carrowmore, pay homage to this one large cairn on Knocknarea. Sixty metres in diameter and ten metres high, it's a beacon for the county and the centre of an ancient ritual landscape. It is instantly recognisable – a miniature version of the mountain itself, set in the coastal grasslands of the Cúil Irra peninsula, with Ballysadare Bay to the south and Sligo Bay to the north. Until recently – indeed since the Stone Age when the cairn was built – the only way to climb to Queen Maeve's cairn was up the old path through the glen, but in the last few years it's become possible, once the old path is climbed, to walk in a loop right around the mountainside, and that's the route I'll take today.

The old path up to the cairn is just over a 300-metre climb – steep but mercifully short. On this unexpectedly hot day, it is popular. There must be a dozen of us on the mountainside – pale men with red faces and their white torsos exposed; young women on their own in summer dresses, in leggings, in shorts. I'm passed by a couple and two dogs – she blonde and striding ahead, he dark and puffing as he walks behind her. Their dogs are as pushy as they are – one runs between my legs as I walk, racing ahead. The couple seem well matched, completing their mission to overtake me just as the path turns left.

In Irish legend, Queen Maeve was renowned for her voracious sexual appetite. The story she is best known for is *The Táin Bó Cúailnge,* or *The Cattle Raid of Cooley*, an epic poem that is part of Ireland's Ulster Cycle of tales. The earliest record of *The Táin* being written down is from the eighth century, but the version we have now dates from the twelfth century onwards and the story is probably many, many centuries older and part of Irish oral storytelling tradition. It begins in Connacht with a quarrel between Maeve and her husband, Ailill mac Máta.

In bed one night, Maeve and Ailill are arguing about who is the richest and decide to compare their wealth. Maeve is incensed to discover that they are equally matched in every way except one – Ailill has an incredibly fertile bull. The bull's name is Finnbennach, the White-Horned, to which none of Maeve's cattle can compare. Not to be outdone, Maeve finds a bull to match Ailill – Donn Cúailnge, the Brown Bull of Cooley, which belongs to Dáire mac Fiachna in Ulster. Maeve sends messengers to Dáire offering enticements of wealth, land and sexual favours – all in return for a loan of the bull. But when a drunken messenger reveals to Dáire that they would have taken the bull by force if they had to, Dáire withdraws from the arrangement. War is declared between Ulster and Connacht. The Connacht army is led by Maeve (who is introduced on the very first page as a warrior), her husband Ailill and her lover Fergus, an Ulster warrior in exile.

Maeve and her Connacht allies have an advantage. The Ulster army is in dire straits – suffering from a curse. Because the king of Ulster forced the goddess Macha to race against a chariot while she was heavily pregnant, Macha has cursed the army to suffer her labour pains. And so, it is left to the seventeen-year-old Ulster hero Cúchulainn to take on the might of Maeve and Connacht. He does this by defeating a series of champions in single combat, assisted and hindered by the gods and goddesses of the Tuatha Dé Danann – a supernatural race of beings who love to interfere in human affairs. In particular, he is both plagued and helped by the Morrigan, a goddess of war, whose advances he spurns before knowing her true identity.

I read Ciaran Carson's immensely enjoyable 2007 translation of *The Táin*, and although the hero is teenage Cúchulainn, I found Maeve magnetic – a determined character of unabashed sexuality, able to persuade all around her to do her bidding. As well as the cattle raids there are chariot fights, beheadings and adultery – Maeve's 'friendly thighs' are often mentioned, and there are bawdy jokes about her lover Fergus's sword. Maeve and Cúchulainn encounter each other throughout, until at last he gains the opportunity to kill Maeve herself. This only happens when she is vulnerable – her period, her 'gush of blood', arrives on the battlefield and she must relieve herself. In the end, Cúchulainn shows his nobility by letting her go free. He is, he says, not in the habit of killing women. Maeve is victorious in capturing the bull Donn Cúailnge, but the rival bulls kill each other, and peace is restored. I found myself annoyed that Maeve had been defeated in battle but also heartened by the mention of her period and her unabashed sexual desire. She seems a formidable character with boldness, passion and agency. I can't help but reflect that the vision of Irish female sexuality presented here is a refreshing one, with an air of freedom and choice.

The entrance to the steep climb to the cairn is marked by a metal kissing gate beside which a sign hangs: 'No Dogs Beyond This Point'. There on a rock sits the man of the couple who overtook me, left behind with the two small brown dogs while his partner completes the trail up to the cairn. I head up the track, which is fast growing steeper and more strenuous. The path becomes rough steps, and on the hillside to the left is a deserted village where a tour guide is explaining to a group of young English people how it was abandoned. I turn and take in the views around me – Ballisadare estuary on the left and the pine forest that covers much of Knocknarea to my right.

The path has been fitted with wooden steps placed into the hillside, beside which purple heather blooms, although at other times of the year the mountain can be covered in coarse yellow gorse. It is part of the beauty of the climb that, despite seeming a barren place, the colour of this hillside changes with the seasons. Benbulben appears to my right as I climb higher. Soon I will be able to see the whole of this side of the county. The ancients who built this cairn knew what they were doing – the pale grey mound of the monument doesn't reveal itself until the last minute: a great ritual reveal for walkers – ancient or modern – making their pilgrimage to the top.

On an earlier visit, I met Dr Stefan Bergh, the archaeologist who has dedicated his career to the understanding of this site and who wrote the explanatory signs posted at various points on the climb. He is currently engaged in a UNESCO world heritage bid to celebrate and manage all the Stone Age monuments on the Cúil Iorra peninsula. Over coffee in Strandhill village, he explained to me that in *The Táin* Maeve is not associated with Sligo – there are, in fact, three or four monuments across Ireland named Miosgán Meadhbha. He can find no record of the cairn being named after Maeve until the 1830 Ordnance Survey map. The Sligo antiquarian Charles O'Conor, who would have visited the site in the 1780s, makes no mention of her.

Stefan explained to me how the cairn is part of an ancient ritual landscape that covers County Sligo. He showed me a map in which lines have been drawn connecting the various ancient sites – from the older monuments at Carrowmore nearby to the Ballygawley Mountains to the east and the Ox Mountains to the south, as well as the passage tombs of my beloved Carrowkeel. These monuments once interacted and paid homage to each other across the mountaintops of the county, reflecting the beliefs of our Stone Age ancestors who lived in the fields beneath them. Incredibly, of the 250 remaining passage tombs in Ireland, 70 are found on Sligo's Cúil Iorra peninsula – of which Maeve's cairn is the star.

On flat-topped Knocknarea itself, Maeve's monument is at the centre of a line of at least five tombs. There is a low platform beneath the cairn, as well as a complex system of banks carved into the eastern side of the mountain. Stefan believes this was a ritual site in late Stone Age Ireland – a place, much like a great cathedral or a monastery, where our ancient ancestors gathered. He believes that it was probably built by a person or family of great social status and that the whole site was, for the pilgrim as they approached, something like a stage set – a highly choreographed place in which different ceremonies were held. We spoke about sites like this in our

202 | Wild Atlantic Women

own contemporary world – Himalayan monasteries, the Vatican, Saint Paul's Cathedral – where various important figures of the past are buried. These are places that reflect who we are, and Queen Maeve's cairn is one of them – a ceremonial monument designed and made to be seen by as many people as possible and celebrate the person interred within.

We can only speculate about what went on here, but some believe that, in a society where most did not live beyond thirty years old, people would have had a great connection with the dead and their ancestors, and that a place like Knocknarea may have provided continuity across the generations – explaining that special feeling I get when I am here. In a time when the daily, monthly and seasonal movements and patterns of the moon, sun and tides of the sea were important, a place like Queen Maeve's cairn provided a fixed mark in the landscape around which all else moved.

I have reached the top of the mountain now, and facing the cairn, I feel it is still a revered site. Knocknarea truly does, in my experience, have a hold on the people of Sligo. People here are proud of the mountain, claiming ownership of it and feeling linked to it. Now that I know it more completely, I wonder if the story of Queen Maeve – of her power, fierceness and sexuality – even if it only became attached to the cairn in later times, is part of why it is still a loved, often visited place.

I have read that the cairn might once have been covered in white quartz from the nearby Ox Mountains, and as I circle it, I notice large chunks of quartz embedded in the ground. But today the cairn is a simple mound of grey limestone. Perhaps part of its appeal is that it has never been excavated – it retains an air of true mystery. The local landlord R. C. Walker threatened to do so in the nineteenth century, but thankfully he never did. That the tomb is intact is key to both its preservation and the legend – for we don't know if Maeve is truly inside, or indeed if anyone is inside at all.

In John Waddell's *Archaeology and Celtic Myth* he puts forward that she may in fact have been a sovereignty goddess – a ritual being representing the land, who kings would marry as they took the throne. Her name is synonymous with 'mead' and may mean 'one who intoxicates'. Having several husbands and several sexual partners is often aligned with this kind of figure. The legend of being buried upright to face your enemies is also an ancient myth belonging to the sixth-century king of Connacht Eoghan Bell, who died in 542 in another great battle – the Battle of Sligo – between Ulster and Connacht. Queen Maeve's story may have been grafted onto his own. He was said to have asked his men to bury him upright inside the ancient cairn, facing his enemies with a red spear in his hand, just as Maeve was said to do.

I leave the monument behind me to begin the loop trail west, passing the large hollow where the stones for the cairn were quarried. Before me, the estuary of Sligo Bay appears – a large marbled surface of water and sandbanks, the wind rippling on the surface of the Atlantic. The trail drops down to reveal the airstrip – the tiny outline of what was once Sligo airport, where my father flew into when my grandmother died. Now I can see the beach at Strandhill, the lighthouse in front of Coney Island and, beyond that, Rosses Point where I swam only yesterday, and Benbulben towering behind it. A glider takes off from the airport as I continue downhill, and as the trail curves north-east, the narrow isthmus of Strandhill comes into view – the main beach on one side, where the surfers play, and on the other, across the sand-dunes, my favourite beach here: the sandy, often deserted Culleenamore.

I've left the walkers of the main climb behind now and am alone on this new trail around the mountain, where more wooden steps have been inset across the hillside. Soon I'm in the forest, grateful for the shade. The forest floor is covered in tree roots, moss and rust-coloured pine needles; the bottom branches of these tall trees are bare and cut short. This is an oppressive place, through which I walk for about twenty minutes – an otherworld of fairy tales, inhabited by now extinct wolves. The wooden pathway ends and now a gravel path takes me along the lower edge of the forest, fringed with what I think are young sycamores. I reflect on Maeve's story – the emphasis on sex, on blood and power, in the legend makes her also feel true. This lack of repression in the main female character of Ireland's national epic has taken me by surprise and I feel renewed. Does it even matter if Maeve existed? Isn't what she symbolises, like Granuaile – a kind of unstoppable feminine force – why she's still remembered?

Past the ruins of a shepherd's house, I come to two gates. The first leads left, straight downhill to the village of Strandhill; the second right, around the lower slopes of Knocknarea and then back to Rathcarrick where I began. It is shaded and solitary – a place to reflect on what Stefan Bergh had been trying to explain when he told me of a conversation he had had with a local farmer who had asked him, 'Is Queen Maeve buried in the mountain?' Stefan told me he had hesitated, unsure of what to reply, before saying yes. For the farmer, he explained, the cairn and mountain had merged, so that both are a monument within which Queen Maeve was buried. I believe this too. Whatever the dates say, whoever is in the cairn, if anyone, doesn't matter. For me, Queen Maeve is in the mountain. She is a part of Sligo's landscape – the two have become one – and somehow I feel closer to her than ever, closer to Sligo and sad to be going back home to London for the winter, to find work and to know that the cold, dark days are coming and it is time to hunker down.

11. COLD WATER MOUNTAINS

Easkey Britton
Rossnowlagh, County Donegal

It's late November before I can make it to Ireland again, and the days are thinner and darker as we move towards midwinter. I arrive in Rossnowlagh at eleven in the morning – the peak of high tide – and park on the clifftop outside the Smugglers' Creek Inn, closed in this quiet season. I'm here in south Donegal for a walk recommended to me by Dr Easkey Britton, a Rossnowlagh native who also happens to be Ireland's most famous big wave surfer. The waves Easkey surfs are the kind that form here on the stormy shores of Donegal, which she calls cold water mountains. A true pioneer, in her teens and twenties she was five times Irish national surf champion. Now, as well as a surfer, she is a marine social scientist, activist and writer, specialising in how we as human beings impact our environment.

I spent yesterday afternoon feeling snug and protected in Easkey's wooden cabin here on the Rossnowlagh shore while she answered my questions about her passion for this coastline. A difficult woman to pin down, it had taken months of toing and froing to finally set up our meeting, but she'd taken my persistence in good humour, making me welcome and even positioning herself so that I had the best view of the ocean as we talked. By the end of our conversation I'd come to think of this landscape in a completely different way. She'd pointed out to me how the Dartry Mountains I'd driven across from Sligo to get here – Benbulben, Benwiskin, Truskmore and Tievebaun – resemble the crests of waves. They have fossils on their limestone summits from when they were once part of the seabed millennia ago. We'd spoken for over an hour about surfing, travelling and water – how we use and how we treat our Atlantic coastline.

After our chat back at the Pier Head Hotel in Mullaghmore – which also happens to be Ireland's most famous big wave surfing beach – I'd intended to spend the evening walking on the strand. Until, that is, Storm Arwen hit, its huge hailstones taking out the power across much of County Sligo as well as the towns of Bundoran, Rossnowlagh and Killibegs. And so I'd spent the hours before bed typing up notes in the bar where people had gathered to keep warm, eating the last hot meal the kitchen could provide by candlelight. Now, having slipped over the Sligo border into Donegal again this morning I'm looking forward to this, my penultimate walk, from a swim spot called The Creek at the southernmost part of the strand, where Easkey told me she and her sister had played as children, along the shoreline of Rossnowlagh to where Durnesh Lough flows into Donegal Bay. Famous for its whooper swans, it's beside this lough, the sluice gate of which is my aim, that Easkey grew up.

I sit and drink a coffee in the car with the radio on and the heating turned up, waiting for the heavy rain, a remnant of the storm, to stop. As I look out on the bay my phone flashes up with messages from Saturday-morning London – a friend's new house where the offer has gone through; a photo of a dog walk in Crystal Palace from a potential boyfriend who I think is not *quite* over his ex; a hello from my best friend sitting in a corridor while her toddler does a ballet class. I've been back in London these last two months, freelancing in television and trying to make sense of what these walks have brought me. At first I found it disorienting. Another single friend in her forties had announced she was leaving – to Brighton this time, so just a train ride away, but still, that made three single friends lost from London now. Was it my imagination or did people's faces seem a little more unhappy and worn out than before? And was it the effects of the city or my own projection? What would my life be like if I left London and came here?

At one point in our conversation, Easkey had told me a scientist friend of hers, Cliff Kapono, was studying how our environment changes us on a biophysical level, on a study he called the surfer biome project. He was asking if the ocean essentially leaves its fingerprint on us in terms of our microbiome. And he found it does. Surfers who surf regularly carry around with them a kind of ocean bacteria that people who live on land all the time don't have. 'So the ocean does actually become part of us as well,' she had told me. People who garden a lot, she mentioned, might have a bio fingerprint of their garden; people who live in the mountains might be changed by the environment there. I thought about it later back in the hotel and realised how much of my life I have spent on the London underground, going back and forth to school and to work – presumably the Tube has changed me on a molecular level.

The rain looks like it's easing off and I change into my boots. Here on the clifftop, I can see the entire bay that I'm about to walk. Leaving the car, I follow the road north, winding round and then down to a small track that leads onto the sand. Walking in winter is different to walking in summer. The rain, the cold – it all hits you more. Just being in this environment in this weather, I am coming to realise quite how hardcore what Easkey does in those big waves actually is.

Surfing was already in the blood of the Britton family when Easkey was born. In the 1960s, Easkey's grandmother Mary Britton had returned from a trip to California with two surfboards that she thought she might offer to the American guests who stayed at her hotel. Instead, her five sons, including Easkey's father, Barry, became some of the first serious Irish surfers. Easkey can't recall the first time, she says, that she stood up on a board – but she would have been very young. She and her sister were always playing in the shorebreak as they became familiar with the waves, and by the age of seven, Easkey was under-eight national champion. She's jealous now of beginners who are learning – of the joy of the first time you get up on your feet and a wave takes you. Easkey can, however, completely recall some of her most memorable wipeouts. 'They tend to stay with you,' she says. 'Not in a bad way, just I guess it's so immersive.' Having been terrified by the power of the Atlantic the couple of times I've taken surf lessons myself, I'm in awe of how she is comfortable surfing within these waves, the force of which can cause serious harm. In her book *Saltwater in the Blood* she speaks about how saltwater and blood taste the same.

There's no surf today and the strand is deserted, the sand almost pristine. I pass Easkey's cabin but the curtains are drawn. The tide is starting to recede and left behind are heaps of glossy seaweed mixed in with brown autumn oak leaves, razor-clam shells and the occasional feather. The sea foam is thick and substantial. In the distance, what I guess is Slieve League – where I trekked a pilgrim trail with friends a few summers ago – is topped with snow. Easkey is unique among the women whose lives I have tried to understand – even Granuaile, who would have sailed these 'cold water mountains' in all kinds of conditions – in that, when she surfs she is completely and utterly at one with the ocean, in conversation with the very waves themselves. Her deep intimacy with the Atlantic is something I am fascinated by.

Protected by the glass walls of her cabin, I asked her if she ever feels that she can see what is going on beneath the waves. She considered my question, looking out at the strand. 'Even at a glance you can tell that it's not going to be good surf today. The wind is blowing onshore and that makes the waves choppy and disorganised; it looks chaotic.' She described for me the best conditions for surfing – a groundswell, where the swell lines spread out in an almost perfectly timed sequence, and no or very little wind. I remarked that she sounded almost like a sailor, a navigator, reading the sea, and she said it's something that comes to her without thinking. Easkey's connection to the sea is so deep, she told me, that when she travels

she gets anxious if she arrives in the night and isn't ori-
entated to the nearest coast and always has to ask those
around her for the direction of the ocean.

As I walk, the day starts to warm up a little. I take photos of the various seaweeds in their winter forms, hoping
to identify them later. I watch the sanderlings or dunlins
– I'm not sure which – as they skitter about; find a smooth
black granite stone with white quartz lines like paint drawn
across it. The water patterns left by high tide reflect the sky
above, so that the sky and beach are a single shining surface, only broken by the mountains in front of me and the
sea itself. I feel the tension in my body release out here in
all this space. A windsurfer with a green sail moves along
the shoreline parallel to me. The sun rises higher in the sky,
and now it is warm enough to stand without gloves – for a
few minutes at a time, at least.

Easkey's teenage years and early twenties were dominated by competitive surfing. In 2007, when she was
twenty-one years old, she became the first female surfer
to ride Aill na Searrach, an infamous big wave off the
Cliffs of Moher. In 2009, she became British Pro-Tour
Champion, and by 2010, when she was twenty-four,
she won her fifth consecutive Irish National Surfing
Championship title at Easkey, County Sligo – the wave
she had been named after. In 2011, Easkey became the
first woman to be nominated for the WSL Big Wave
Awards, for tow-surfing at Mullaghmore.

As a teenager, she told me, her body was seen as
something to overcome in surfing – staying on the pill
continuously to repress any hormonal variations when
she was competing. An Irish surf coach told her when
she was fourteen that she 'had to surf more like a guy,

to be more aggressive'. I asked her if, as her fame grew, she felt more pressure because of her gender. 'I think I wasn't exposed to it very much because I grew up surfing with the lads or family, but then with big wave surfing, it did become a thing I noticed. That my gender was really singled out at the time.'

She found it odd, she says, as the appeal of big wave surfing for her was partly that it stripped away identity. 'You're so exposed,' she told me. 'It's just you and the elements. And so that's what I felt when I found big wave surfing initially. I felt like, this is so amazing – this total freedom from self or identity or ego in those moments.' The way Easkey speaks, I can imagine how completely, how evangelically, her passion for riding big waves grew once she discovered it. But this idea of being singled out because of her gender, when in fact in her surfing she felt she had discovered a way to escape the boundaries of gender, of identity even, touches a nerve with me.

Many times throughout writing this book I have worried that I'm limiting the people I am writing about, these great scientists, artists, writers, sailors, surfers, by categorising them all together in this way as women – as if I am Ellen Hutchins sorting and labelling a species. Through researching their lives, I have come to understand how individual everybody's path is. That there are no rights or wrongs or set formats in life. I believe that people are people, complete and themselves, above their gender. I tell Easkey how tangled I feel about this, because while I feel identity is completely individual, I also have to contemplate the fact that life was different, is different, if you are a woman moving through this landscape.

Options were limited for women of the past on this coastline, wearing the necessarily bulky clothing of yesteryear, weighing up their marriage chances without a dowry or trying to keep a family together when their husbands were away at sea. And even today, when I have more freedom than any generation of women before me, I have had to weigh up risk – whether I am putting myself in peril by being alone, by walking alone.

'Because it is different, actually,' says Easkey. 'The experience is different.'

Easkey went on to tell me about her film, *A Lunar Cycle* – an exquisitely shot meditation on solitude in which she rides the waves of this western coastline. She told me that her intention was to make a film with a feminine perspective, as an antidote to all the hyper-masculine 'wave porn' surfing films she was encountering at film festivals. As I did on the Blaskets, when I met Lesley Kehoe, I know that I am on the right path again, talking to Easkey, an understanding that researching and recording women's stories is important.

I reach the end of the strand, now approaching what I think must be the start of the estuary. The sand beneath me has become dotted with stones and small shells and the air smells danker. The sun dims, then reappears. Large pools have formed around the rocks on the shoreline, sometimes deeper than they first appear, and if I'm not careful I might find my feet soaked. The pieces of seaweed sometimes look like insects or like shrimp with vertebrae and arms. And now the ground is covered in heaps of sandworm casts. I cross what is almost like a field of thick stripped kelp, drying orange and yellow and brown, that Easkey said they used to chew on in the summer as kids.

As time went on, Easkey decided to compete less and less, becoming instead a free surfer, travelling the world riding different waves, often being photographed or filmed. Surfing became a passport through which she would be welcomed by communities across the globe – places like Indonesia, Fiji, Tahiti and the Mentawai Islands. Slowly, as she travelled, she began to see the impact that unsustainable surf tourism was having across the world. 'It felt very extractive. Foreign, Australian or American owned boat charters setting up these resorts to create the illusion of surf paradises, of perfect waves. Dropping anchor everywhere and probably creating a lot of wastage. There was just very little integration – at the time, anyway. It all started to feel off to me as a professional surfer.' Even when marine conservation was happening, she felt, it was often foreign agencies coming in to perform it, rather than the local people who had been living with the ocean for centuries – their knowledge and wisdom frequently ignored.

Easkey began studying to become a marine social scientist, specialising in the relationship between people and the sea. I ask her what inspired her to pivot, and she says, in part, it was the emotional bond that she had formed with the ocean – the part of her story that most fascinates me. She studied environmental science first, at the University of Ulster in Coleraine, partly because it was a fieldwork-based degree with lots of marine modules and also because she could live in Portrush and continue to surf. At first she thought she might become a marine conservationist, studying coral reefs, but eventually she came to realise that the human dimension to marine conservation was key to her work. 'Needing to restore our relationship with it, I saw as the actual issue.' She's gone on to make our relationship with water the focus of her career. Her books *50 Things to Do by the Sea* and *Saltwater in the Blood* both speak about reciprocity with the ocean – how we are interdependent on it, how it is the life-support system for our planet, how marshes, wetlands, sea grasses and mangroves absorb more carbon than forests on land and produce much of our oxygen.

Easkey's number one concern about Ireland's coastline is water quality. 'It's all connected,' she told me. Ireland, being such a small island, is criss-crossed with waterways and rivers and lakes, all flowing into the ocean. 'We need to make a connection that whenever we come into water, it's having a knock-on effect. When we touch water, we're impacting it, affecting it, changing it, and therefore changing the ocean.' She explained to me how, in the twenty-first century, raw sewage outflow is still such a problem in both Ireland and the UK. Over half of Ireland's rivers and lakes are unsafe to bathe in or fish. Easkey spoke to me about how we celebrate our beautiful Wild Atlantic Way in terms of tourism, pulling in money with our incredible coastal resource. 'There's a total commodification of the ocean and it's extremely disrespectful at the very least ... it's a kind of hypocrisy, to make money out of wildness but for it not to be clean.'

Her words impacted me. I felt ready to hear what she had to say – I had come a long way from when I started my travels, when I too had become captivated by this image of the Atlantic coastline as a wild place. I have plundered this shoreline too, with my Ryanair flights and my mileage up and down the coast, and I was glad I'd been able to speak to her, to look into this mirror.

Presumably, I asked Easkey, she could have studied or lived anywhere in the world. What drew her back to Donegal, apart from family? 'That's a good question,' she answered. 'Because it does have this almost gravitational pull, considering the incredible places I've been and the opportunity I've had to travel. But I haven't found anywhere like Donegal – it has this rugged wildness, rawness to it. You get that all along the west coast of Ireland, but there's something particularly in Donegal that's just sort of totally unrefined.' She spoke about the rock, the limestone and granite, the changeability of the weather. 'And it's also the most incredible concentration of surfable waves nearly anywhere in the world,' she said smiling. 'There's something about that constant motion and energy and change, being really shaped by the weather here, more than anywhere I've been.'

I round the corner to a small cove as the rain begins again, walk round another bay. Always, I begin to realise, when the light has a certain yellow shadowy beauty, it means the rain is coming. On the last bay of my walk, a sign tells me to leave the upper path – that it is private property. Past the entrance to a holiday park, I make my way off the strand and up some wooden steps, into the dunes, where I climb up as far as I can before a fence forbids me from going any further. But no matter, because in front of me is my aim, Durnesh Lough, on the other side of which Easkey grew up. On the lake I can see a multitude of whooper swans, here to nest for the winter. I am happy, but the wind is howling. I sit down in the dunes for shelter and take a rest.

Easkey is part of an initiative at Durnesh Lough, she told me, to improve the water quality locally. It's a unique habitat for birds and waterfowl – especially herons and the whooper swans I can see in the distance. But this last summer it was covered in an algal bloom, and what with low water levels, the sluice gate wasn't working properly. The intention of the work she's part of is to build a sense of stewardship and connection to it as a place, to try to understand what it means to people. She spoke about being aware and conscious when we are outside in our natural environments – something that, I hope, I am beginning to do myself.

The rain finally stops and I turn back the way I came. No sooner have I rounded the corner of the bay than Easkey and her father, Barry, appear before me. I immediately feel like some kind of fan-girl stalker, even though we've been exchanging messages for months. I explain to them that I wasn't sure how far to go. 'Oh, I'm so sorry,' says Easkey, 'I should've sent you a pin drop,' while her father tells me that I should really walk all the way to Donegal town. He jokes that I could hitch-hike back. 'Where are you from anyway?' asks Barry, and when I tell him East London, for some reason it sounds so funny here on this beach, with not a soul but ourselves about, that he responds with a brilliant laugh.

What must it be like, I wonder, as I walk back across the main strand, to know this landscape as intimately as Easkey and her dad? To have this continuation with the same place, day after day? It's why, I guess, my mum and dad wanted to return to Sligo, to live along the lane to where my dad grew up, whereas I never now go to the suburban London street on which I was born. Why would I? It's just another street of 1930s houses like all the rest. There's a different family living there now, whereas the lane in Sligo is a place we've been connected to for over a hundred years.

For my thirtieth birthday a group of friends and I visited Sligo, and they had been amazed by the fact that my grandparents are buried a few hundred metres away – in the churchyard around the corner. I realised then that some people don't have that – a connection with a physical place that is home in a bigger sense, not just the house you were born or grew up in. But then, even though I've moved addresses half a dozen times, London creates this connection somehow too – this feeling of each individual life being part of a larger story, as the city constantly renews itself. Perhaps I don't need to move anywhere – perhaps, for now anyway, I have it just the way it works? Two places, London and Sligo, both of which can have equal status as home.

The tide is out now, and the shells crack beneath my feet as I head back along the middle bay and then onto the main strand of Rossnowlagh. Passing by Easkey's cabin, I think about what she told me when we were discussing the ongoing effects of climate change, which I can't help but have noticed on my travels – the more extreme weather on Aran; the industrial cutting of the kelp in Bantry; the erosion of the sand-dunes along the Connemara coast. She pointed out of the cabin window to a place where a grass bank, in her mother's time, extended out by another twenty metres. 'But there's massive erosion, and even here that bank – in my time – has receded … You can't stop that.' This landscape is constantly moving, shaping and reshaping, she says. That's just part of the natural order, to some extent – but there are things we could do: sort out our water quality and educate children to have an awareness, a respect and a wonder for the Atlantic Ocean that I myself, on these walks, have only just begun to nurture.

EPILOGUE: DUE NORTH

Malin Head, County Donegal

Six months have passed since that wintry day on Rossnowlagh Beach and the year has turned; spring passed into summer so that now it is June and I am walking from Ballygorman to Malin Head. My walk today will take me to the tip of Donegal and the northernmost point of Ireland, part of a circle around the top of the Inishowen peninsula. Orange as well as yellow dandelions grow by the roadside here and, as I put one foot in front of the other, I recall the slow, comforting monotony of the shipping forecast, thinking to myself that I am in one of those places that has always seemed so far away.

My conversation with Easkey had given me much to think about. We'd spoken about the masculinity of the coastline, about historic attitudes to the sea in Ireland. About the history I have learnt researching this book – the men away fishing, the wakes for children going to America, the stories of shipwrecks, of the monks on their islands seeking closeness with God. 'I mean,' Easkey had said, 'this sea was probably more a place of loss and grief and danger and something worth forgetting in our collective psyche in Ireland until relatively recently.' She was right, of course. We talked about Peig Sayers shouting at her children to keep them from the shore.

But within the stories of the individual women in whose landscapes I walked, there was also hope. Studying the botany of the seashore had given both Ellen Hutchins and Maude Delap purpose and freedom; the Aran landscape had provided the Aran knitters with inspiration; the Atlantic waves had allowed Granuaile to become a mythic force. Even in the deep sadness of emigration, I found that the women who left in the 1800s for America were, for the most part, happier in their new lives. Opportunities opened for them.

I stop in at a curiosity shop on the side of the road. The old man who owns it is busy with another customer, but when they leave he turns his attention to me. The shop is full of bric-a-brac – old shaving jugs and Guinness memorabilia, road signs and Toby jugs. Soon we're deep in conversation about who I am and where I'm going; how business is; how the tourists are this year. He jokes that my metal water bottle must contain whiskey as I'm in such good spirits, and the ice broken, I tell him my name – as always my passport into acceptance. We agree that Sligo, like Donegal, is a beautiful but underrated county. I buy nothing, which I later regret, wishing I had kept some memento.

When I started this journey, walking alone in rural places was new to me. I am used to navigating city streets, to planning my routes around the dangers they can have for women, but walking along this coastline was different. I wondered at times if it was foolish, dangerous even, to walk solo along clifftops and through fields and forests I did not know. I decided in the end that it was important to do what I wanted – important for us, collectively, as women to do what we want. Other women I met travelling alone felt similarly and I found, too, that they were almost all interested in the lives of the women who had come before them.

Many times I felt overwhelmed by the task I had set myself and worried that I could not do it justice. But the power of the Atlantic and the beauty of this coastline carried me along, as in exploring their paths I found both inspiration and purpose. I began to feel that I knew the women – Ellen Cotter's capability; Ellen Hutchins's intelligence and work ethic; Kate O'Brien's middle-class gentility, while all the while leading an incredibly non-conformist life. I revelled in the brilliance of Edna O'Brien's writing and in Queen Maeve's unabashed sexuality, and was intimidated by my namesake Granuaile and her ruthless warrior nature. I came particularly to love Maude Delap, the rector's eccentric daughter, at work in her homemade laboratory, sending violets to her unrequited love in London.

And of course, I thought a lot about Peig Sayers, her sharp memory and the sadness of losing her children. With time, I have come to enjoy the occasional eye roll that accompanies her name and I think of her very affectionately. I was pleased to make what I hope will be a lasting connection with Úna on Inisheer and to meet Easkey Britton, who brought me a full circle in terms of thinking of identity and femininity and how women are seen. Easkey had also helped me contemplate my own personal responsibility towards nature and this coastline. Concentrating on the lives of these women, consciously and unconsciously, allowed me to experience Ireland in a way I never had before, locating me in both time and space. Through their stories, I acquired an Irish history and geography that I had been lacking – a history of great resilience. It also brought me closer to my parents, spending so much time in Sligo as I came and went doing these walks.

At times, and still now, I felt like an imposter with no right to tell these stories when I wasn't born in Ireland. Sometimes I worried that I was exploiting, for my own means, the women of this book and this Atlantic landscape. Sometimes I felt the outsider, that I was in a space in which I didn't belong. I came to understand how ignorant I had been of Ireland's history and, through that ignorance, a little more about the complex tensions that exist between the two nations that I am privileged in being able to move between. They are thoughts that are appropriate here, in Donegal, where Scotland seems only a stone's throw away and the Irish border is just a couple of hours' drive.

Everything here on the tip of Ireland is 'most northerly' – Farren's Bar declares itself Ireland's most northerly bar and opposite the signal tower is Ireland's most northerly coffee shop, staffed by an ever-patient man in a small kiosk that protects him from the wind, serving tourists as they come and go. I check with him where the most northerly point really is, and he directs me right. To get down to the cliffs, I climb over a wooden stile, fighting the wind as I follow the track that curves around the headland to the cliff edge. I walk across the

Éire 80 sign – the four letters and two numbers made of stones cemented together and painted white, a relic from World War II, a message to pilots that they had entered neutral territory.

I sit down on the rocks as near to the edge as I dare. This, then, is Banba's Crown, named after one of Ireland's most ancient patron goddesses, whose sister Ériu gave her name to Éire. On this green, springy ground, the cliffs drop as if the land has been torn up beneath me. Just six feet away is the deep crack that separates the mainland from the last large grassy outcrop of the peninsula. In front of me lies the remote island of Inishtrahull, made of gneiss, the oldest rock in Ireland, and beyond is Tor Beg – a rocky outcrop that is the last torn piece of Ireland before what mapmakers have named the North Atlantic Ocean begins. If I look east, I can see a faint smudged line in the very, very far distance – the hills of western Scotland. I try, as I have done along this entire journey, to spot the basking sharks that live in this water but see only the rise and fall of tiny white crests of waves, the restlessness of the sea reflecting my own choppy, fragmented thoughts.

The longer I have spent on this coast, the less 'wild' it has seemed. Familiarity overturned some of my preconceptions about what remote places are, about what wildness is. By walking for many hours, I began to appreciate with each step the diversity and variety of this Atlantic landscape. To experience some reciprocity with nature – a feeling that my behaviour was accountable when it came to looking after, not only this coastline, which has been shaped by centuries of Atlantic erosion, but also the planet of which it is only one small part. Walking in this landscape also made me begin to realise the immense freedom I have, in the twenty-first century, as a woman to live as I like, to walk where I want.

It's taken many months and a lot of reading and thinking to really understand whether and how much these walks have changed me as a person. It's a process that I'm still undergoing. Engaging with and writing about the lives of each of these women helped me work out how trapped I had been by my own idealised version of how an average woman's life should go. To realise that, like each of the women in whose lives I wandered, my life has its own unique shape that is, of course, subject to the vagaries of circumstance. This might seem obvious now – after all, I had chosen to follow women who had, in different ways, lived unconventional lives. But when I began, I don't think I understood what it was that I was searching for.

When I set out, I did not anticipate the level of commitment I would need to truly engage with the lives of each of these distinct people and what they could teach me. But the more walking I did, the more work I did, and the more I got back. It was worth it, as I gained an acceptance of my own life. To understand that it's OK not to have hit what other people see as life milestones and that any anxieties I have about not yet having a partner and children are just feelings that will pass. After all, I have my own life milestones, and one of them has been exploring the lives of the women in this book. It has been an experience that has given me so many hours of joy, as together these women and this landscape helped me grow and nurtured my confidence.

I pull my hood up around me and watch the hypnotic surface of the waves as they rise and fall. It is clear to me now that the Atlantic ocean is alive, a constant beyond time and beyond the lives of any of the women in this book. An eternal body of water that connects Ireland to the rest of the world. In the distance there is a streak of blue light, of a sun-filled sky beyond the unbroken whiteness of the clouds overhead. I begin to feel impermanent, as I did on the Great Blasket – a person passing through. The waves crash against the headland, becoming turquoise and translucent as they wash. Four birds – cormorants – flap their wings dry before they take off. I stand and continue my walk.

ACKNOWLEDGEMENTS

I consulted a great many sources for this work for which I would like to thank the authors or archives in question. Firstly, thank you to Éamon Lankford for his history of Cape Clear and publication and research around my great-grandfather John K. Cotter's life and poetry, without which this book would not exist. I'm also grateful to Siobhán O'Sullivan and Nora Finnegan at the Lace and Design Centre in Kenmare.

Sincere thanks to Madeline Hutchins for her generosity of time and thought and for allowing me to access and publish excerpts from her family letters written by Ellen Hutchins. I am also very grateful to the Master and Fellows of Trinity College Cambridge for permission to quote from letters between Ellen Hutchins and Dawson Turner. Thanks also to the archives at Kew Gardens and the Linnean Society, London.

I am grateful to Anne Byrne and Dr Nessa Cronin for their research around the life of Maude Delap, and to the artist Dorothy Cross for inspiring me with her work.

Thank you also to Jane Sheehan, whom I met on my journey, for explaining to me the basics of marine science, and special thanks to Joanna Lee, Maude Delap's grandniece, for permission to publish excerpts from the unpublished memoir 'Memories of a Loving Alien' by Peter Delap. Thank you to Pam Twentyman at the Valentia Heritage Centre; Amy Geraghty and Aidan O'Hanlon at the Natural History Museum, Dublin; as well as the archives of the Natural History Museum, London, where I gained access to Maude Delap's diaries and logbooks.

I would like to acknowledge and thank the Educational Company of Ireland for granting me permission to use excerpts from Peig Sayers's autobiography *Peig* and Oxford University Press for permission to quote from *An Old Woman's Reflections*. Thank you to the British Library, British Newspaper Archives for access to Charlotte Grace O'Brien's 'Horrors of an Emigrant Ship' in the *Pall Mall Gazette*, 6 May 1881. For access to emigrants' letters I would like to thank the Irish National Archives and the Deputy Keeper of the Records, Public Record Office of Northern Ireland for allowing me to cite Mary Hanlon's letter to Vere Foster from 16 October 1865 – D3618/D/25/10. Thank you also to Dr Críostóir Mac Cárthaigh of the Irish Folklore Collection for allowing me to excerpt from the following: archival reference NFC 1408 p. 172, letter from Mary Brown of County Wexford to her friend (also called Mary), New York, March 11, 1858.

Heartfelt thanks to Edna O'Brien for inspiring me and millions of women like me with her writing. Thank you to Caroline Michel and Kieron Fairweather at Peter Frasers Dunlop for allowing me to quote from *Mother Ireland*. Thank you to Simon McCallum and the BFI for the preservation of the 1976 documentary *Mother Ireland*, which they hold in their archive. My appreciation also to Darragh O'Donoghue at the Tate Archives for allowing me to publish excerpts from his writing about the Tate collection.

To Georgia Glover at David Higham Associates I owe special thanks for allowing me to include excerpts from Kate O'Brien's *My Ireland* and to the *Spectator* magazine for permission to quote from Kate O'Brien's 1951 article for them, 'Connemara'. I am also deeply indebted to Eibhear Walshe for his elegantly written and comprehensive biography of Kate O'Brien, which provided me with many hours of pleasure.

Thanks to the National Archives, Kew, London for allowing me to consult and quote from Sir Henry Sidney's letter to Sir Francis Walsingham, SP: 12/159 f. 27d, and Granuaile's Petition to Queen Elizabeth I, July 1593. Thank you also to Anne Chambers for her incredible biography of Granuaile to which I am very much indebted. I am very grateful to the Dúchas Schools' Collection, which provided me with hours of enjoyable research as I travelled the coastline and researched the lives of the women in this book.

Thanks also to the many people who hosted me or kept me company on my journey, including Irene Harrington in Ahillies, Helen Richmond in Cahersiveen, Ally McKenzie on the Great Blasket Island and Eileen at Seagrove House in Roundstone, Christina Lowry and Bill and Denise Whelan.

To my ever-supportive friends Stephen Burgen, Sarah Coleman, Annabel Hobley, Lisa Mac Hale, Ella St John McGrand, and my readers: Marco Crivellari, Stacey Epler, Imogen Garner, Angela McAllister, Jyoti Mehta, John Mullen, Charlie Outhwaite and Morag Tinto.

I am deeply indebted to my editor Emma Dunne and commissioning editor Aoife K. Walsh at New Island Books for supporting and believing that this book was possible.

Very special thanks indeed are due to Easkey Britton, Dr Stefan Bergh, Lesley Kehoe and Úna McDonagh, who gave their time and words so generously and supportively.

Finally, thank you to my parents, my sister Anna Faulkner, cousin Orla Jackson, Con and Monica O'Shea, Jean and Bill Foley and all of my wider family – both Cotter and Lyons – for their steadfast support in the research and writing of this book.

BIBLIOGRAPHY

Anbinder, T. (2016). *City of Dreams: The 400-Year Epic History of Immigrant New York*. Boston: Houghton Mifflin Harcourt.

Another Island: A Portrait of the Blasket Islands (1984). Documentary, Dublin, RTÉ.

Armstrong, J. S. (1910). 'The Lace Industry of Ireland', *Daily Consular and Trade Report*, Washington, Wednesday 5 October 1910, no. 79, issued by the Bureau of Manufactures, Commerce and Labour.

Bartlett, T. and J. Kelly (2018). *Cambridge History of Ireland 1730–1830*. Cambridge: Cambridge University Press.

Bergh, S. (2017). *Neolithic Cúil Irra, Co. Sligo – Knocknarea, Carrowmore, Carns Hill*, Archaelogy Ireland, Heritage Guide no. 78, NUIG. Dublin: Archaeology Ireland.

— (1995). *Landscape of the Monuments: A Study of the Passage Tombs in the Cúil Irra Region*. Stockholm: Riksantikvarieämbetet Arkeologiska undersökningar.

Britton, E. (2021). *50 Things to Do by the Sea*. London: Pavilion.

— (2021). *Saltwater in the Blood: Surfing, Natural Cycles and the Sea's Power to Heal*. London: Watkins.

Bunreacht na hÉireann (1937). Article 41.2. Dublin: Oifig an tSoláthair.

Carson, C. (2007). *The Táin: A New Translation of the Táin Bó Cúailnge*. London: Penguin.

Chambers, A. (2018). *Grace O'Malley: The Biography of Ireland's Pirate Queen, 1530–1603*. Dublin: Gill Books.

Cook, J. (2021). *Pirate Queen: The Life of Grace O'Malley 1530–1603*. Edinburgh: Birlinn.

Cooney, G. (2000). *Landscapes of Neolithic Ireland*. London and New York: Routledge.

Cotter, J. K. (2016). *Ó Charraig Aonair go Droichead Dóinneach: From Fastnet Sound to Blackwater Bridge of Youth and Prime and Life and Time – Poems by John K. Cotter*, compiled and edited by Éamon Lankford. Cork: Celum Publishing.

Cronin, N. (2017). 'Maude Delap's Domestic Science: Island Spaces and Gendered Fieldwork in Irish Natural History', *Coastal Works: Cultures of the Atlantic Edge*. Oxford: Oxford University Press.

Delaney, C. 'Peig'. *The Irish Examiner*, 10 March 2021.

Delap, M. (1901). 'Notes on the Rearing of *Chrysaora isosceles* in an Aquarium', *The Irish Naturalist* 10: 25–28.

— (1899-1909). 'Log Book (Diary) of Mrs M. J. Delap, Given on a Visit to her Home on Valencia', Natural History Museum Collections, London.

Delap, P. 'Memoirs of a Loving Alien', private memoir provided by Valentia Island Heritage Centre.

Diner, H. R. (1983). *Erin's Daughters in America: Irish Immigrant Women in the Nineteenth Century*. Baltimore: Johns Hopkins University Press.

Fairbarn, H. (2016). *Ireland's Wild Atlantic Way: A Walking Guide*. Cork: The Collins Press.

Finnegan, N. and E. (2013). *The Lace Story: Kenmare and Other Irish Laces*. Kenmare Lace Festival.

Flower, R. E. W. (1944). *The Western Island; or, the Great Blasket*, with illustrations by Ida M. Flower. Oxford: Clarendon Press, 1944.

Foster, V. (1855). *Work and Wages; or the Penny Emigrant's Guide to the United States and Canada for Female Servants, Laborers, Mechanics, Farmers & Co.* London: W. & F. G. Cash.

Griffin, W. D. (1981). *The Irish in America*. Dublin: Academy Press.

Gwynn, S. (1909). *Charlotte Grace O'Brien: Selections from her Writing and Correspondence with a Memoir by Stephen Gwynn*. Dublin: Maunsel and Co., Ltd.

His Majesty's Stationery Office (1909). *Eighteenth Report of the Congested Districts Board for Ireland*. Dublin: Cahill & Co.

Hull, E. (1912). *The Poem Book of the Gael: Translations from Irish Gaelic Poetry into English Prose and Verse*. London: Chatto & Windus.

Hutchins, E. and D. Turner (1999). *Early Observations on the Flora of Southwest Ireland: Selected Letters of Ellen Hutchins and Dawson Turner 1807–1814*. Dublin: National Botanic Gardens.

Hutchins, M. (2019). *Ellen Hutchins (1785–1815) Botanist of Bantry Bay*. Ellen Hutchins Festival (in association with the Bantry Bay Historical and Archaeological Society).

'Journalist with Long and Varied Career', Veronica Thomas obituary. *The Irish Times*, 27 August 2011.

Kanigal, R. (2012). *On an Irish Island*. New York: Alfred A. Knopf.

Kenny, M. 'The Most Hated Woman in Irish History'. *The Irish Independent*, 3 May 2008.

Langan, T. (1990/1). 'The Congested Districts Board', *The North Mayo Historical Journal*, 2.3.

Lankford, É. (1999). *Cape Clear Island: Its People and Landscape*. Cape Clear Museum.

Levey, S. (1983). *Lace: A History*. London: Victoria and Albert Museum.

Lewis, S. (1837). *A Topographical Dictionary of Ireland*. London: S. Lewis & Co.

MacIntyre, J. (1976). *Three Men on an Island*. Belfast: Blackstaff.

Mahon, B. (1998). *While Green Grass Grows: Memoirs of a Folklorist*. Cork: Mercier Press.

Man of Aran (1934). Film, director R. J. Flaherty.

Miller, C. (1996). 'Tumbling into the Fight: Charlotte Grace O'Brien (1845–1909), the Emigrant's Advocate'. *History Ireland*, 4.4.

Mother Ireland (1976). Documentary, LWT for ITV, now held by BFI Archive.

Mulkerns, V. (undated). 'Kate O'Brien: A Memoir'. *The Stony Thursday Book*, Vol. 7. Limerick: Arts Office of Limerick City Council (cited in Walshe, E.).

Mulvihill, M. (1997). *Stars, Shells and Bluebells: Women Scientists and Pioneers*. Dublin: Women in Technology and Science.

Murray, A. E. (1903). *History of the Commercial and Financial Relations between England and Ireland from the Period of the Restoration*. London: P. S. King.

My Own Place: Edna O'Brien Comes Back to County Clare (1975). Documentary, Dublin, RTÉ.

O'Brien, C. G. (1881). 'Horrors of an Emigrant Ship'. *Pall Mall Gazette*, 6 May 1881.

O'Brien, E. (1960). *The Country Girls*. London: Hutchinson.

— (1976). *Mother Ireland*, with photographs by Fergus Bourke. London: Weidenfield and Nicolson.

— (2012). *Country Girl: A Memoir*. London: Faber and Faber.

O'Brien, F. (1973). *The Poor Mouth*, translated by Patrick C. Power, illustrated by Ralph Steadman. London: Grafton.

O'Brien, K. (1940). *Mary Lavelle*. London: William Heinemann, Chatto & Windus.

— (1962). *My Ireland*. London: B. T. Batsford.

— (1953). *The Flower of May*. London: William Heinemann.

— (1958). *The Land of Spices*. London: Hamilton & Co.

— (1946). *That Lady*. London & Toronto: William Heinemann.

— (1958). *As Music and Splendour*. London: Heinemann.

— (1951). 'Connemara'. *The Spectator*, 16 November.

O'Cleirigh, N. (1992). *Valentia: A Different Irish Island*. Dublin: Portobello Press.

Older and Wiser (1973). Radio interview, RTÉ (cited in Walshe, E.).

Reynolds, L. (1987). *Kate O'Brien: A Literary Portrait*. Gerrards Cross: Colin Smythe.

Sayers, P. (1978). *An Old Woman's Reflections*, translated from the Irish by Séamus Ennis and introduced by W. R. Rodgers. Oxford: Oxford University Press.

— (2009). *Labharfad le Cách: Scéalta agus Seanchas Taifeadta ag Radio Éireann agus BBC/I Will Speak to You All: Stories and Lore Recorded by Radio Éireann and the BBC*, edited by Bo Almqvist and Pádraig Ó Héalaí. Dublin: New Island Books.

Solnit, R. (1997). *A Book of Migrations: Some Passages in Ireland*. London: Verso Books.

Verschoyle, J. (1866). 'The Condition of Kerry', *Living Age*, 171.

Waddell, J. (2014). *Archaeology and Celtic Myth*. Dublin: Four Courts Press.

Walshe, E. (2006). *Kate O'Brien: A Writing Life*. Dublin: Irish Academic Press.

GRÁINNE LYONS is a writer and documentary-maker from London, where she lives. She holds an MA in Creative and Life Writing from Goldsmith's University and a BA in English Literature from the University of York. Her work has been published in *The Irish Times* and *Aesthetica* magazine and she was shortlisted for the *Mslexia* first novel competition in 2017. As a documentary producer, she has produced numerous arts and history films. Gráinne's family live in her father's home place of County Sligo, where she lives when she's not in London. @grainne_lyons